Fabulous Flip Pan Cookbook

Fun easy recipes by Debra Murray

Contents

I would first like to thank my incredible daughter, Nevar Murray. From the moment she came into this world, she has inspired me to do better every day. I am so proud of the beautiful young woman she has become. Nevar has the same passion for food as myself; whether it be to eat or prepare, food is one of the foundations of our relationship. Thank you Nevar for inspiring me to try new cuisines and always reach higher.

I want to thank my mom, Yvette, and my dad, Reggie, who have loved, supported, and encouraged me my whole life. I have achieved what I have in life because of your love and support.

The person I need to thank the most is my dear friend and buyer, Mark Linduski. I am so grateful to Mark for asking me to join his team at a new TV network. My heart skips a beat every time a new invention comes to my home and I love bringing them to life for you on TV. Thank you Mark for this opportunity; doing what you love is by far one of the sweetest gifts of life!

A huge thank you to Curtis Anderson, the owner of Course Housewares; who invented the Flip Pan. The Flip Pan is by far one of my favorite cooking tools of all time. Thank you for making this book possible and all the support you give me.

To my incredible Facebook group for the Flip Pan, I wake up every morning to see the delicious photos in my news feed of all your creations. You all show so much love and support for one another with your shared passion of cooking. Thank you Josephine Cook, for working constantly to help everyone and answer any questions that arise. Josephine, you are a true life angel!

As for my amazing team who helped make this book a reality. Thank you, Erin White for being my live TV wing woman, Brenda Torre for being my TV makeup artist, Susan Livingston for being my book designer, Suzi Hammond for letting me use your kitchen for the cover, and Deanna Hawk for doing my make up for the cover. Last but not least to two of the best girl friends; Laurie Ingram Bain and Yilldred Tortosa. Not only did you two style and shoot all the spectacular photos for this book, you both have been my friends over two decades. I am so blessed to have both of you.

I have been blessed with so many friends who nurture and inspire me every day. Thank you to each and every one, to mention them all I would need another book . . .

Tips for Success with Flip Pans

The Flip Pan, when closed by the magnet, is two pans attached with a gasket, which will retain 90 percent of the cooking steam, turning the pan into a low-pressure pressure cooker. This means you will retain more flavor and more nutrients than cooking with other pans. You will also experience faster cooking times. In this book I have included 100 different recipes some for the Jumbo Flip Pan others for the Original Flip Pan.

What is low pressure cooking, approximately 3 PSI. This is when the cooking liquid or the moisture from the food you are cooking creates steam, by prohibiting the escape of the steam it reduces cooking time over a conventional covered pot—water boils at a higher temperature under pressure, thus speeding up the cooking process. Plus, bathing food in steam seals in flavor and nutrients that are typically boiled out on the stovetop. So with the Flip Pans you get better tasting, juicier, meals faster!

The first thing I always recommend and the manufacturer will as well, clean your Flip Pan with Soap and water, towel dry, then I rub or season the ceramic surface with olive oil. The ceramic is a fabulous chemical free nonstick, but it is water based. Like any water based product, occasional seasoning of the surface will give your surface a longer life. To have optimum release I do recommend a nonstick spray; in the grocery stores there are tremendous new products like pump not aerosol nonstick sprays which are healthy like Grape seed and Coconut oil. Most of my recipes will call for preheated without oil or spray, top and bottom. But I am a person who will never leave that pan unattended. If you find you are a person who may leave the pan in the preheat stage, I recommend adding oil to the pan so the nonstick does not turn brown. I heat my pan till I feel the heat coming off the pan, then I add my spray or my oil.

I know we call the Flip Pan a flip pan; but that does not mean everything needs to be flipped. Do not flip if adding cooking liquid, because of the steam hole, this will create a mess on your stove, plus the added weight could cause the pan to open while turning.

My favorite technique is to brown the protein on both sides, flipping if using the original Flip Pan, then add my liquids such as stock or wine. As for the Jumbo Flip Pan, I only flip when making kettle corn.

How to get the best results when cooking proteins. Typically I keep the Flip Pan closed for most dishes, except steak, tuna or scallops. The first thing I do when cooking any protein is I make sure the poultry, steak, pork, fish or seafood is very dry, all residual moisture removed.

I let my proteins sit at room temperature for at least 20 minutes. Then I rub my proteins with just enough oil to adhere the seasonings I will put on them. Then I make sure the pan is hot; I love to begin with a couple minute sear per side on medium high, then I back the temperature to medium. As I mentioned before, steak, tuna and scallops I will cook the entire piece 90 percent before closing the lid for the last minute or two to infuse with a cooking liquid. The other meats I like to preheat the Flip Pans top and bottom then cook, say for a chicken breast I cook 5 minutes per side.

How do I calculate how long to cook the meat. This is not an exact science, but I have found that if I preheat the pan top and bottom, and because of the seal of low pressure the pan creates closed, I take all typical cook times and cut in half. If a recipe calls for pork chops to cook 10 minutes per side for ½ inch pork chops. I automatically would cook them for 5 minutes per side. Every now and again, I wish I had cooked them a bit less or I need to give them a few minutes longer. But 90 percent of the time that is the perfect calculation.

I am including a chart in this book, the chart will give you a basic time line and whether or not to use liquid. I calculate you should add 1 tablespoon of cooking liquid for every minutes an item is cooking, unless I have noted not to add liquid at all.

I am so happy you have purchased our fabulous pan and I hope you have as much joy using it as myself and all my wonderful friends in the Flip Pan Group on Facebook. I have asked some of my most loyal recipe posters to contribute to this Flip Pan book.

Love,
Debra Murray

Cooking Chart for Flip Pans

Here is a basic cooking guideline for proteins, vegetables, pasta and rice. I did not include sandwiches, since these would depend on thickness and would not follow a chart, and there are sandwich recipes in this book you could use as a guideline.

When reading the chart, under Cooking Time note that PS means *per side*. If you are using the original Flip Pan you would flip the pan; if using the jumbo Flip Pan you would open the pan and flip the food, then re-seal.

FOOD	THICKNESS/ WEIGHT	COOKING TEMPERATURE	COOKING TIME	LIQUID NEEDED	DONENESS
Steak	1–1½ Inch	Med/High	3–4 Min PS	No	Med Rare
Pork Chops	1–1½ Inch	Medium	10 Min PS	Yes	Well
Chicken	1–1½ Inch	Med/High	5 Min PS	Choose	Well
Burgers	1–1½ Inch	Med/High	4–5 Min PS	No	Med/Well
Sausages	1 Pound	Med/High	5 Min PS	Yes	Well
Salmon	1 Pound	Med/High	3 Minutes	No	Well
Fish Filets	1 Pound	Med/High	2 Min PS	Yes	Well
Bacon	6 Strips	Medium	3 Min PS	No	Med
Shrimp	1 Pound	Medium	3 Min PS	Choose	Med/Well
Eggs	2 Large	Medium	2 Min PS	No	Runny
Ham Steak	1 Inch	Med/High	3 Min PS	No	Well
Drumsticks	1 Pound	Med/High	7 Min PS	Choose	Well
Chicken Thighs	1 Pound	Med/High	8 Min PS	Choose	Well
Spatchcock	3 Pound	Med/High	12 Min PS	Choose	Well
Bb Ribs	½ Slab	Med/High	15 Min PS	Yes	Well
Spare Ribs	6 Ribs	Med/High	20 Min PS	Yes	Well
Pot Roast	3 Pounds	Medium	3 Hours	Yes	Well
Pork Roast	3 Pounds	Medium	2½ Hours	Yes	Well
Cornbeef	3 Pounds	Medium	4 Hours	Yes	Well
Potatoes	2 Pounds	Med/High	20 Minutes	Yes	Tender

FOOD	THICKNESS/ WEIGHT	COOKING TEMPERATURE	COOKING TIME	LIQUID NEEDED	DONENESS
Zuchini	1 Pound	Med/High	3 Min PS	No	Done
Onions	1 Pound	Med/High	4 Min PS	No	Tender
Asparagus	1 Pound	Med/High	2 Min PS	Yes	Tender
Corn	4 Ears	Med/High	4 Min PS	Yes	Tender
Artichokes	2 Halved	Med/High	10 Min PS	Yes	Tender
Green Beans	1 Pound	Med/High	9 Minutes	Yes	Tender
Broccoli	1 Pound	Med/High	4 Minutes	Yes	Tender
Brussels Sprouts	1 Pound	Med/High	10 Minutes	Yes	Tender
Carrots	6–7 Medium	Med/High	7 Minutes	Yes	Tender
Eggplant	1 Medium	Med/High	5 Min PS	No	Tender
Kale	1 Pound	Med/High	8 Minutes	Yes	Tender
Mushrooms	1 Pound	Med/High	4 Min PS	Yes	Tender
Peppers	2 Medium	Med/High	3 Min PS	No	Tender
Winter Squash	2 Pounds	Med/High	12 Minutes	Yes	Tender
Pasta	2 Cups Dry 4 Cups Boiling Liquid	Med/High	8–10 Minutes	Yes	Al Dente
Rice, White	2 Cups Dry 3 Cups Boiling Liquid	Medium	15 Minutes	Yes	Fluffy
Quinoa	2 Cups Dry 2 Cups Boiling Liquid	Medium	12 Minutes	Yes	Fluffy

Recipes for Your Flip Pan

Jumbo Flip Pan
10–67

Original Flip Pan
68–150

Jumbo Flip Pan
Breakfast and Treats

Apple Upside Down Cake

Serves 6

Warm and delicious

INGREDIENTS

½ cup unsalted butter
4 apples, peeled, cored and sliced
½ cup light brown sugar
1 tablespoon Karo syrup
1 box spice cake mix
3 large eggs
1 cup apple cider
⅓ cup vegetable oil
nonstick spray

DIRECTIONS

Preheat oven to 350 degrees

Using only the deep bottom of the jumbo Flip Pan. Place it on a medium burner. Add the butter, apples brown sugar and syrup cook for 5 minutes.

Mix the cake mix with eggs, cider, and oil. Mix till smooth and free of lumps.

Spray pan with nonstick spray. Pour batter over the apple mixture place on the center rack in the oven.

Cook for 30 minutes or till a toothpick comes out clear of batter when stuck in deepest spot of cake.

Let cool for several minutes then invert onto square platter or cutting board.

Serve warm with caramel ice cream

NUTRITION FACTS

Serving Size: ⅙ of a recipe

AMOUNT PER SERVING	% DAILY VALUE
Calories: 390	20%
Calories from Fat: 253	38%
Total Fat: 29g	45%
Saturated Fat: 2g	10%
Cholesterol: 112mg	37%
Sodium: 146mg	6%
Total Carbohydrates: 32g	11%
Fiber: 3g	12%
Sugars: 20g	
Protein: 2g	4%
Vitamin A:	13%
Vitamin C:	4%
Calcium:	1%
Iron:	2%

Cinnamon Swirl Pancakes with Cream Cheese Icing

Serves 4

INGREDIENTS

4 tablespoons melted, butter
¼ cup plus 2 tablespoons light brown sugar
¼ teaspoon cinnamon
pastry bag or freezer bag
2 cups pancake batter
1 plastic squeeze tube
nonstick spray
1 container cream cheese frosting

DIRECTIONS

Mix the butter, brown sugar and cinnamon together, put into a pastry bag, or put it in the corner of a freezer bag, cut a small hole for the swirl to come out about ¹⁄₁₆ of an inch.

Prepare pancake batter, place into squeeze bottle with large hole for a tip. Or better yet a pancake dispenser.

Heat your Flip Pan top and bottom over medium heat, spray with nonstick spray. Squeeze the pancake batter onto griddle side of Flip Pan in 3 inch circles, squeeze the cinnamon mixture onto the pancakes in swirls. After 3 minutes flip the pan cook for 3 minutes longer.

Repeat with remaining batter.

Microwave the frosting for 35 seconds on high, stir and then pour over stacks of pancakes.

To really kick it over the top, add crumbled bacon!!

NUTRITION FACTS

Serving Size: ¼ of a recipe

AMOUNT PER SERVING	% DAILY VALUE
Calories: 145	7%
Calories from Fat: 100	15%
Total Fat: 11g	17%
Saturated Fat: 0g	0%
Cholesterol: 30mg	10%
Sodium: 90mg	4%
Total Carbohydrates: 12g	4%
Fiber: 0g	0%
Sugars: 12g	
Protein: 0g	0%
Vitamin A:	8%
Vitamin C:	0%
Calcium:	0%
Iron:	0%

Kettle Corn

Sweet n Savory Delight

INGREDIENTS

¼ cup vegetable oil

½ cup popcorn kernels

⅓ cup sugar

¾ teaspoon sea salt

DIRECTIONS

Preheat jumbo Flip Pan top and bottom over medium heat for 5 minutes.

Add the oil and increase heat to medium high heat for 3 minutes.

Add the popcorn salt and sugar. When the popcorn starts popping keep shaking the pan to distribute the salt and sugar.

When the popping slows to less from a pop a second to almost a minute. Stop shaking and remove from the heat.

NUTRITION FACTS

Serving Size: ¼ of a recipe

AMOUNT PER SERVING	% DAILY VALUE
Calories: 180	37%
Calories from Fat: 485	73%
Total Fat: 57g	87%
Saturated Fat: 8g	40%
Cholesterol: 0mg	0%
Sodium: 1842mg	77%
Total Carbohydrates: 69g	23%
Fiber: 1g	5%
Sugars: 64g	
Protein: 1g	1%
Vitamin A:	0%
Vitamin C:	0%
Calcium:	0%
Iron:	1%

Jumbo Flip Pan
Side Dishes

Artichokes in Lemon

INGREDIENTS

2 large artichokes

1 tablespoon olive oil

½ cup white wine

½ cup chicken stock

1 tablespoon of fresh lemon juice,
   plus the juice and zest of a large lemon

1 sprig thyme

3 whole peppercorns

DIRECTIONS

Split the artichokes vertically, remove the bottom leaves, and using a potato peeler peel the stem, then using a spoon remove the inner fibers at the center of the artichoke

Place the artichokes in a bowl of ice water with a tablespoon of fresh lemon juice.

Preheat the Flip Pan on medium heat for 2 minutes.

Add the olive oil and heat it for 2 minutes.

Add the artichokes with cut side down and cook for 3 minutes.

Add the remaining ingredients and cook for 10–15 minutes depending on the size of the artichokes.

When cooking is complete, serve the artichokes hot with some of the broth with a few tablespoons of butter added to dip the leaves in.

NUTRITION FACTS

Serving Size: ½ of a recipe

AMOUNT PER SERVING	% DAILY VALUE
Calories: 99	5%
Calories from Fat: 63	9%
Total Fat: 7g	11%
Saturated Fat: 1g	5%
Cholesterol: 0mg	0%
Sodium: 558mg	23%
Total Carbohydrates: 6g	2%
Fiber: 0g	0%
Sugars: 0g	0%
Protein: 1g	2%
Vitamin A:	0%
Vitamin C:	0%
Calcium:	0%
Iron:	0%

Braised Kale

Delicious and healthy!

INGREDIENTS

1 tablespoon olive oil

2 cups thinly sliced, onions

1 teaspoon salt

12 turns freshly ground black pepper

½ teaspoon red pepper flakes

2 tablespoons minced, garlic

8 cups firmly packed kale leaves, torn and stemmed

2 cups basic chicken stock

splash cider vinegar

DIRECTIONS

Place the Flip Pan on the stove on medium high heat.

Add the oil to pan and let heat for 1 minute, add the onions, salt, pepper, and red pepper flakes and stir-fry for 2 minutes.

Add the garlic, kale, and stock and cook, stir to combine, close Flip Pan and cook for 8–10 minutes

Add a splash of cider vinegar in the last minute of cooking.

Remove from the heat. Serve immediately.

Deb's Tip: I like to sprinkle with dried cranberries

Cook Time: 12 minutes

NUTRITION FACTS

Serving Size: ¼ of a recipe

AMOUNT PER SERVING	% DAILY VALUE
Calories: 50	3%
Calories from Fat: 35	5%
Total Fat: 4g	6%
Saturated Fat: 1g	5%
Cholesterol: 0mg	0%
Sodium: 947mg	39%
Total Carbohydrates: 1g	0%
Fiber: 0g	0%
Sugars: 0g	0%
Protein: 3g	5%
Vitamin A:	0%
Vitamin C:	0%
Calcium:	0%
Iron:	0%

Braised Purple Cabbage

INGREDIENTS

2 medium granny smith apples peeled, cored, and chopped coarse

1 small head red cabbage, quartered, cored, and sliced ¼ inch thick

½ cup apple cider

1 cup chicken stock

1 teaspoon light or dark brown sugar

2 teaspoons apple cider vinegar

1 teaspoon salt

DIRECTIONS

Preheat Flip Pan bottom over medium heat for 2 minutes.

Place all the ingredients in the pre heated Flip Pan. Cook over medium heat for 30 minutes.

Cabbage will be tender and flavorful. You may wish to add sliced kielbasa or raisins for extra flavor.

NUTRITION FACTS

Serving Size: ¼ of a recipe

AMOUNT PER SERVING	% DAILY VALUE
Calories: 54	3%
Calories from Fat: 0	0%
Total Fat: 0g	0%
Saturated Fat: 0g	0%
Cholesterol: 0mg	0%
Sodium: 593mg	25%
Total Carbohydrates: 13g	4%
Fiber: 2g	8%
Sugars: 4g	
Protein: 0g	0%
Vitamin A:	0%
Vitamin C:	3%
Calcium:	0%
Iron:	0%

Potato Salad

INGREDIENTS

3 ½ pounds small creamer potatoes, scrubbed
1½ cups water
½ teaspoon sea salt
3 large eggs
1 tablespoon kosher dill pickle juice
¼ cup minced sweet onion
2 ribs celery, minced
½ teaspoon celery seed
½ teaspoon celery salt
½ teaspoon fresh ground pepper
½ cup mayonnaise
1 teaspoon yellow mustard
chives, for garnish

DIRECTIONS

Place the water, potatoes and salt in Flip Pan.

Close the lid and bring to a boil, lower heat to medium and cook for 20 minutes.

Add the eggs to the Flip Pan with the potatoes and cook 5 minutes longer.

Place eggs in a bowl of cold water, and drain the potatoes and allow to cool.

In a large bowl, mix the onions, celery and potatoes and toss with pickle juice.

Peel and dice the cooled eggs and add to the potatoes.

Add the remaining ingredients, mix well and serve chilled.

NUTRITION FACTS

Serving Size: ¹⁄₁₅ of a recipe

AMOUNT PER SERVING	% DAILY VALUE
Calories: 76	4%
Calories from Fat: 5	1%
Total Fat: 1g	2%
Saturated Fat: 0g	0%
Cholesterol: 29mg	10%
Sodium: 126mg	5%
Total Carbohydrates: 15g	5%
Fiber: 2g	8%
Sugars: 1g	
Protein: 3g	5%
Vitamin A:	1%
Vitamin C:	21%
Calcium:	3%
Iron:	2%

Jumbo Flip Pan
Soups and Stews

Fresh Vegetable Soup

INGREDIENTS

½ cup sweet onion, diced

3 garlic cloves, sliced

¼ cup celery, diced

¼ cup carrot, peeled and sliced

¼ cup celery root, peeled and diced

¼ cup green beans, cut into ½-inch pieces

¼ cup fresh corn

¼ cup Brussels sprouts, diced

1 can (14.5 ounces) petite diced tomato

3 cups beef broth

1 spring thyme

1 teaspoon sea salt

1 teaspoon freshly ground pepper

1 cup cooked pasta or quinoa

DIRECTIONS

Place all ingredients except pasta into the Flip Pan; close the lid.

Set on medium heat and set a timer for 20 minutes.

When cooking is complete add in the pasta serve immediately.

I love drizzling pesto into my vegetable soup.

Cook time: 20 minutes

NUTRITION FACTS

Serving Size: ⅙ of a recipe

AMOUNT PER SERVING	% DAILY VALUE
Calories: 94	5%
Calories from Fat: 4	1%
Total Fat: 0g	0%
Saturated Fat: 0g	0%
Cholesterol: 0mg	0%
Sodium: 1362mg	57%
Total Carbohydrates: 17g	6%
Fiber: 1g	4%
Sugars: 1g	
Protein: 6g	11%
Vitamin A:	14%
Vitamin C:	4%
Calcium:	1%
Iron:	6%

Chicken Pho

INGREDIENTS

8 cups low-sodium chicken broth (two 32-ounce boxes)

2 tablespoons light brown sugar

2 tablespoons fish sauce

4 wholes cloves

1 medium onion, quartered

1 2-inch piece fresh ginger, peeled and thinly sliced

1 tablespoon coriander seeds

2 bone-in chicken breasts, skin removed, trimmed

6 ounces wide rice noodles

2 cups mung bean sprouts

2 cups fresh basil leaves

1 cup fresh mint leaves

1 cup fresh cilantro leaves

1 fresh serrano, thinly sliced

1 lime, cut into 6 wedges

4 scallions, thinly sliced

NUTRITION FACTS

Serving Size: ⅙ of a recipe

AMOUNT PER SERVING	% DAILY VALUE
Calories: 968	48%
Calories from Fat: 83	12%
Total Fat: 9g	14%
Saturated Fat: 2g	10%
Cholesterol: 9mg	3%
Sodium: 3117mg	130%
Total Carbohydrates: 31g	10%
Fiber: 1g	4%
Sugars: 5g	
Protein: 12g	22%
Vitamin A:	2%
Vitamin C:	46%
Calcium:	0%
Iron:	2%

DIRECTIONS

Place the Flip Pan on the stove and set to medium high heat.

Combine broth, brown sugar, fish sauce, cloves, onion, ginger and coriander into Flip Pan.

Add chicken breasts, meat-side down. Cover and cook for 2 hours over medium with lid closed.

Transfer the chicken to a cutting board. Remove spices and discard.

Add noodles, cover and cook for 30 minutes.

Remove the chicken from the bone and shred with two forks. When the noodles are tender; stir in the shredded chicken.

Serve bowls of soup with bean sprouts, basil, mint, cilantro, sliced chili, scallions and lime wedges on the side so everyone can add their own toppings.

Total Cook Time: 2.5 hours

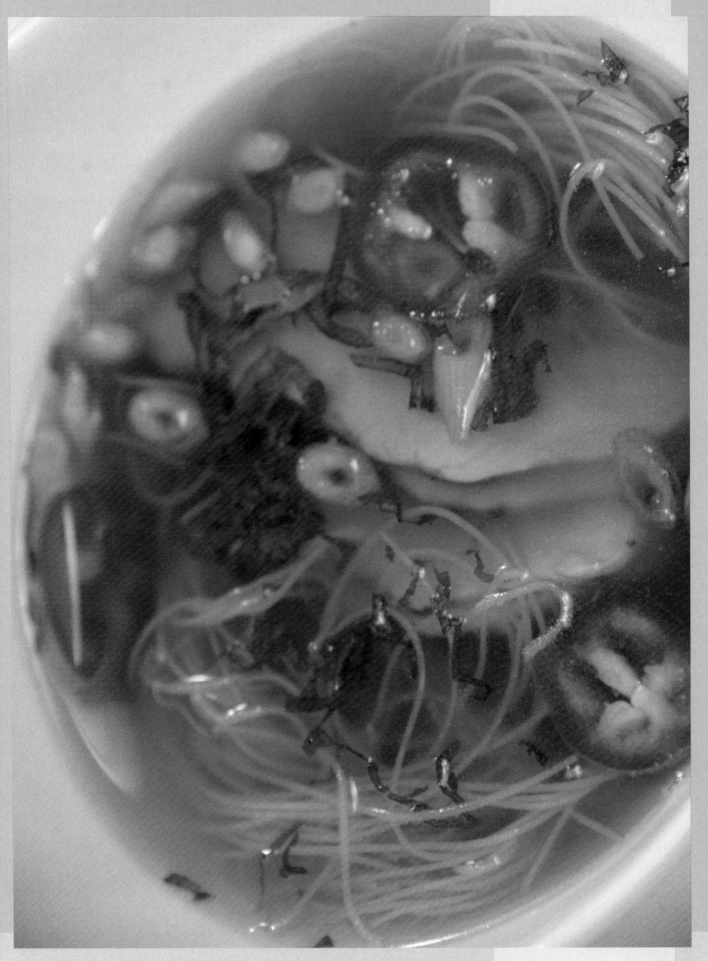

Chili Verde

INGREDIENTS

2 dried chilies, seeded and chopped

7 tomatillos

1 4-ounce can green chili, diced

1 cup chicken stock

1 tablespoon of olive oil

3 pounds pork loin, cubed

1 green chili, coarsely chopped

1 jalapeno, diced, seeds and membrane removed

1 onion, coarsely chopped

4 garlic cloves, minced

1 teaspoon cumin

1 teaspoon salt

1 teaspoon ground pepper

1 bundle cilantro, chopped with stems removed

sour cream

NUTRITION FACTS

Serving Size: ⅛ of a recipe

AMOUNT PER SERVING	% DAILY VALUE
Calories: 251	13%
Calories from Fat: 86	13%
Total Fat: 10g	15%
Saturated Fat: 4g	20%
Cholesterol: 90mg	30%
Sodium: 1304mg	54%
Total Carbohydrates: 3g	1%
Fiber: 1g	4%
Sugars: 0g	0%
Protein: 39g	71%
Vitamin A:	1%
Vitamin C:	3%
Calcium:	0%
Iron:	4%

DIRECTIONS

In a food processor or blender, add dry chilies, tomatillos and can of green chilies and chicken stock puree.

Place the Flip Pan on the stove on medium high heat let heat for 2 minutes.

Add the oil heat for 2 minutes.

Add the pork and brown on all sides. About 5 minutes. Add the jalapeño, onion, garlic, cumin, salt and pepper and stirring cook for 5 minutes longer.

Add the pureed mixture, stir then close the Flip Pan lid set burner to medium to medium low.

Cook for 1 hour, stirring occasionally.

When cook time is complete, serve hot in bowls topped with a dab of sour cream and chopped fresh cilantro.

Beef Stew

Delicious hearty stew . . .

INGREDIENTS

2 medium garlic cloves, minced

4 anchovy fillets, finely minced

1 tablespoon tomato paste

1 boneless beef chuck roast (about 2 pounds),
   trimmed of excess fat, cut into 1½-inch pieces

salt and pepper

2 tablespoons vegetable oil

1 large onion, halved and diced

4 medium carrots, peeled and cut into 1-inch pieces

¼ cup unbleached all-purpose flour

2 cups red wine

2 cups beef broth

1 bay leaf

1 sprig fresh, thyme

1 pound Yukon gold potato, scrubbed and cut into 1-inch pieces

1½ cups frozen pearl onions, thawed

NUTRITION FACTS

Serving Size: ¼ of a recipe

AMOUNT PER SERVING	% DAILY VALUE
Calories: 212	11%
Calories from Fat: 61	9%
Total Fat: 7g	11%
Saturated Fat: 1g	5%
Cholesterol: 2mg	1%
Sodium: 947mg	39%
Total Carbohydrates: 31g	10%
Fiber: 4g	16%
Sugars: 1g	
Protein: 7g	13%
Vitamin A:	331%
Vitamin C:	26%
Calcium:	3%
Iron:	6%

DIRECTIONS

Mash the anchovies, garlic, and tomato paste together well. Preheat the jumbo Flip Pan over medium heat.

Add the oil. When the oil is hot, about 2 minutes, season the beef chunks with salt and pepper.

Add the beef chunks and cook all sides till a rich brown in color.

When meat has finished browning. Add the flour and stir till smooth.

Stir in all the other ingredients stir, and close the lid and set timer for 1 hour.

When cooking is complete discard the bay leaf and thyme.

Josephine's Italian Vegetable Stew (Ciambotta)

Serves 5

Ciambotta is a stew that we grew up with. Whatever veggies, we had went into the pot.

INGREDIENTS

2 cloves garlic, cut up
2 large cut up stalks of celery
   (I like to add some of the celery leaves, too)
3 medium cut up potatoes
2 large cut up carrots
1 large cut up onion
2 medium cut up zucchini
1 pound of cleaned string beans
fresh basil, about 4 large torn leaves
8 ounce can of no-salt tomato sauce
1 teaspoon salt
¼ teaspoon black pepper
1 tablespoons olive oil
5 cups veggie broth

NUTRITION FACTS

Serving Size: ⅕ of a recipe

AMOUNT PER SERVING	% DAILY VALUE
Calories: 151	8%
Calories from Fat: 4	1%
Total Fat: 1g	2%
Saturated Fat: 0g	0%
Cholesterol: 0mg	0%
Sodium: 1271mg	53%
Total Carbohydrates: 34g	11%
Fiber: 8g	32%
Sugars: 6g	
Protein: 7g	13%
Vitamin A:	141%
Vitamin C:	35%
Calcium:	6%
Iron:	9%

DIRECTIONS

Preheat the Jumbo Flip Pan on low heat for 3 minutes on each side

Open the lid and in the deep side add the oil

Raise temperature to medium low and add the garlic and onions

Close the lid, sweat the onions and garlic for 5 minutes.

Open the lid add the carrots, celery, celery leaves, basil, potatoes, salt, pepper, water and tomato sauce, raise the heat to medium.

Close the lid, cook for 30 minutes

Open the lid add the string beans, close the lid and cook for 10 minutes

Open the lid and add the zucchini, cook 4 minutes.

Check your salt and pepper, add if needed

TIP: when cooking stews and soups, the well on the Flip Pan fills up, so before opening I take a paper towel and dab the liquid.

Lentil Turkey Sausage Soup

Serves 4

INGREDIENTS

1 pound sweet Italian turkey, sausage, cut into 1-inch pieces
1 medium onion, diced
2 garlic cloves, sliced
1 large carrot, peeled and thinly sliced
1 celery stalk, thinly sliced
1 cup lentils
2 cups beef stock
1 can (14.5 ounces) diced tomatoes with garlic and olive oil
1 bay leaf
½ teaspoon crushed red pepper flakes (optional)

DIRECTIONS

Place Flip Pan on medium high burner and preheat 2 minutes.

Add the sausage and brown with lid closed for 2 minutes.

Add in the onion and cook with lid closed for another 2 minutes.

Add the garlic and stir, add in the remaining ingredients.

Close the lid, lower to medium heat and cook for 20 minutes.

When cooking time is complete, discard the bay leaf and serve immediately.

Cook Time 30 Minutes

NUTRITION FACTS

Serving Size: ¼ of a recipe

AMOUNT PER SERVING	% DAILY VALUE
Calories: 656	33%
Calories from Fat: 413	62%
Total Fat: 46g	71%
Saturated Fat: 17g	85%
Cholesterol: 147mg	49%
Sodium: 1394mg	58%
Total Carbohydrates: 23g	8%
Fiber: 10g	40%
Sugars: 1g	
Protein: 32g	58%
Vitamin A:	83%
Vitamin C:	7%
Calcium:	1%
Iron:	34%

Coconut Chicken Soup

Flavorful Delicious Soup

INGREDIENTS

1 teaspoon sesame oil

1 shallot, minced

2 cloves garlic, minced

1 teaspoon fresh grated, ginger

1 teaspoon lemongrass minced

2 teaspoons red curry, pasta

1 can coconut milk, 13.5 ounces

1 tablespoon brown sugar

1 cup fresh bean sprouts

1 small jalapeno, seeded, membrane removed and sliced thin

3 cups chicken stock

1 red bell pepper, julienned

2 cups rotisserie chicken, meat shredded

zest and juice from 1 lime

1 teaspoon soy sauce

½ teaspoon Siracha (optional)

¼ cup of fresh cilantro, leaves chopped

NUTRITION FACTS

Serving Size: ¼ of a recipe

AMOUNT PER SERVING	% DAILY VALUE
Calories: 102	5%
Calories from Fat: 23	3%
Total Fat: 3g	5%
Saturated Fat: 0g	0%
Cholesterol: 13mg	4%
Sodium: 666mg	28%
Total Carbohydrates: 8g	3%
Fiber: 1g	4%
Sugars: 4g	
Protein: 13g	24%
Vitamin A:	0%
Vitamin C:	35%
Calcium:	1%
Iron:	1%

DIRECTIONS

Preheat the jumbo Flip Pan on medium heat for 3 minutes.

Put the oil in the Flip Pan and heat.

After 2 minutes add the onion, garlic and ginger and lemongrass and curry paste close lid and let sweat for 5 minutes.

Stir in all the remaining ingredients except the cilantro.

Close the Flip Pan and cook for 25 minutes.

When cook cycle is complete stir in cilantro.

Thai Chicken Noodle Soup

Serves 4

INGREDIENTS

1 tablespoon vegetable oil

1 onion, thinly sliced

2 cloves garlic, minced

2 tablespoons green curry paste

6 cups low-sodium chicken broth

1 15-ounce can coconut milk

1 tablespoon fish sauce, plus more to taste

2 red bell peppers, thinly sliced

4 ounces thin rice noodles, broken into pieces

2 small skinless, boneless chicken breasts (about 1 pound), very thinly sliced crosswise

1 tablespoon fresh lime juice, plus more to taste

1 cup roughly chopped fresh cilantro

DIRECTIONS

Heat the vegetable oil in a jumbo Flip Pan over medium-high heat.

Add the onion and cook, stirring occasionally Close lid and cook for 2 minutes.

Add the garlic and curry paste and cook, stirring, then close lid and cook 1 to 2 minutes.

Add the chicken broth, coconut milk and fish sauce; Close the lid and cook for 5 minutes.

Add the bell peppers and noodles and simmer, uncovered, until the noodles are al dente, about 3 minutes.

Add the chicken close the lid and cook 3 more minutes.

Stir in the lime juice and cilantro. Add more fish sauce and lime juice, if desired.

Cook Time: 25

NUTRITION FACTS

Serving Size: ¼ of a recipe

AMOUNT PER SERVING	% DAILY VALUE
Calories: 1099	55%
Calories from Fat: 134	20%
Total Fat: 15g	23%
Saturated Fat: 4g	20%
Cholesterol: 14mg	5%
Sodium: 3449mg	144%
Total Carbohydrates: 26g	9%
Fiber: 0g	0%
Sugars: 0g	0%
Protein: 15g	27%
Vitamin A:	2%
Vitamin C:	7%
Calcium:	0%
Iron:	2%

29

Jumbo Flip Pan
One Pot Wonders

Buffalo Chicken Cheese "Steak"

INGREDIENTS

2 4-ounce boneless skinless chicken breasts
1 tablespoon olive oil
1 teaspoon salt
½ teaspoon pepper
1 medium onion, sliced thin
1 red bell pepper, julienned
¼ cup wing sauce
4 slices provolone cheese
2 Italian hoagie rolls
2 teaspoons ranch dressing
2 tablespoons crumbled blue cheese
½ cup shredded iceberg lettuce
1 small tomato, sliced
sliced hot pepper (optional)

DIRECTIONS

Heat Flip Pan over medium heat for 2 minutes. Pat the chicken breasts dry with a paper towel.

Season with salt and pepper, add oil to the Flip Pan and preheat for 2 minutes; add the chicken breasts.

Cook for 4 minutes with lid closed then flip and cook 2 minutes longer. After 2 minutes add in the onions and peppers, cook for 3 minutes with lid closed.

Remove the breasts from the pan and slice very thin on a cutting board and then add back into the pan with the onions and peppers.

NUTRITION FACTS

Serving Size: ½ of a recipe

AMOUNT PER SERVING	% DAILY VALUE
Calories: 331	17%
Calories from Fat: 222	33%
Total Fat: 26g	40%
Saturated Fat: 13g	65%
Cholesterol: 62mg	21%
Sodium: 1815mg	76%
Total Carbohydrates: 6g	2%
Fiber: 2g	8%
Sugars: 0g	0%
Protein: 21g	38%
Vitamin A:	23%
Vitamin C:	30%
Calcium:	54%
Iron:	2%

Continued >>

Leave the pan on the burner but turn off the heat. Cover with the glass lid and now use the jumbo Flip Pan grill pan to toast the hoagie rolls.

Place the provolone cheese on the meat and then cover the pan with a lid.

After you toast the rolls; spread the ranch on the rolls.

Divide the chicken onion cheese mixture between the rolls, drizzle with the wing sauce.

Top with shredded lettuce and tomatoes and blue cheese crumbles.

Buffalo Chicken Macaroni n Cheese

Serves 4

INGREDIENTS

6 frozen chicken tenders
3 cups dry pasta
3 cups chicken stock
1 small onion, minced
1 stalk celery, minced
1 small carrot, minced
½ cup of buffalo wing sauce, divided
½ cup whipped cream cheese
1 cup medium cheddar, shredded
1 cup mozzarella, shredded
½ cup Parmesan cheese, grated
½ cup crumbled blue cheese
French fried onion

DIRECTIONS

Place the stock in the jumbo Flip Pan and bring to a boil over medium high heat.

Add the chicken tenders, pasta, onion, celery and carrots to Flip Pan and close the lid.

Set timer for 12 minutes.

When cook time is complete open Flip Pan, stir in the cream cheese and half the wing sauce, add in the remaining cheeses, and stir till smooth.

To serve, scoop mac n cheese into serving bowl, sprinkle with blue cheese crumbles, drizzle with wing sauce and top with crunchy fried onions.

NUTRITION FACTS

Serving Size: ¼ of a recipe

AMOUNT PER SERVING	% DAILY VALUE
Calories: 652	33%
Calories from Fat: 128	19%
Total Fat: 14g	22%
Saturated Fat: 6g	30%
Cholesterol: 124mg	41%
Sodium: 1072mg	45%
Total Carbohydrates: 66g	22%
Fiber: 4g	16%
Sugars: 3g	
Protein: 73g	133%
Vitamin A:	85%
Vitamin C:	15%
Calcium:	26%
Iron:	21%

Chicken with
Sweet Potato Dumplings

Serves 4

INGREDIENTS

chicken stew

6 chicken thighs, bone-in, without skin

1 teaspoon salt

1 teaspoon freshly ground pepper

½ teaspoon fresh rosemary leaves, chopped

1 tablespoon extra-virgin olive oil

¼ cup white wine

1 cup chicken stock

½ cup pearl onion

1 celery stalk, sliced

1 large carrot, peeled and sliced

1 sprig thyme

dumplings:

2 ¾ cups unbleached all purpose, flour

1 cup mashed sweet potato

½ teaspoon salt

2 teaspoons baking powder

5 ½ cups buttermilk

garnish:

1 tablespoon fresh parsley, chopped

¼ cup tiny frozen peas, thawed

NUTRITION FACTS

Serving Size: ¼ of a recipe

AMOUNT PER SERVING	% DAILY VALUE
Calories: 679	34%
Calories from Fat: 164	25%
Total Fat: 19g	29%
Saturated Fat: 6g	30%
Cholesterol: 79mg	26%
Sodium: 1914mg	80%
Total Carbohydrates: 92g	31%
Fiber: 2g	8%
Sugars: 17g	
Protein: 14g	25%
Vitamin A:	197%
Vitamin C:	10%
Calcium:	44%
Iron:	22%

DIRECTIONS

Season both sides of the chicken thighs with salt, pepper and rosemary.

Place the Flip Pan on medium high burner for 2 minutes, add the oil and heat a couple minutes longer.

Season the chicken with salt and pepper and add to the Flip Pan and brown well on both sides approximately 3 minutes per side with lid open.

Add the wine, stock, pearl onions, celery, carrots and thyme to the Flip Pan and close the lid.

Set timer for 20 minutes.

While cooking, combine all dumpling ingredients in a bowl; mix but don't over mix.

When cooking is complete, discard the thyme.

With lid open makes sure stew is simmering.

While simmering, drop dumplings by the spoonfuls to the Flip Pan.

Cook the dumplings for 3 minutes on each side with lid closed. Use a slotted spoon to turn.

Cook time: 31 minutes

Delicious Chicken n Dumplings

Tender comfort food in under 30 minutes

INGREDIENTS

4 bone-in chicken breasts, skinless
1 tablespoon olive oil
½ teaspoon salt
½ teaspoon pepper
1 small onion, diced
1 can condensed chicken soup
2 cups frozen mixed veggies
1 7-ounce container pop n fresh, biscuit dough
parsley

DIRECTIONS

Place the jumbo Flip Pan on medium heat to preheat.

Add oil to Flip Pan and season the chicken breasts with salt and pepper.

Brown the chicken breasts skin side down with lid open about 4 minutes till nice and brown.

Add the onion and stir.

Close the Flip Pan and cook for 5 minutes.

Add the remaining ingredients except the biscuit dough and cook for 10 minutes.

Top with biscuit dough. Close lid and cook for 5 minutes longer.

Garnish with parsley

NUTRITION FACTS

Serving Size: ¼ of a recipe

AMOUNT PER SERVING	% DAILY VALUE
Calories: 206	10%
Calories from Fat: 59	9%
Total Fat: 7g	11%
Saturated Fat: 1g	5%
Cholesterol: 27mg	9%
Sodium: 846mg	35%
Total Carbohydrates: 24g	8%
Fiber: 1g	4%
Sugars: 2g	
Protein: 14g	25%
Vitamin A:	0%
Vitamin C:	5%
Calcium:	0%
Iron:	10%

Cantonese Shrimp with
Lo Mein Noodles

Serves 4

INGREDIENTS

1 pound jumbo shrimp, peeled and deveined

2 tablespoons sesame oil

1 tablespoon fresh ginger, minced

2 cloves of garlic, minced

½ cup stir fry sauce

1 red bell pepper, julienned

1 cup broccoli flowerets

4 green onions, chopped

1 teaspoon crushed red pepper flakes

1 cup cooked Lo Mein noodles

DIRECTIONS

Place the Flip Pan onto burner, over medium high heat

Let Flip Pan heat for 2 minutes.

Add the shrimp and cook for 3 minutes with lid closed, flip then cook 3 minutes longer.

Add the sesame oil ginger and garlic. Close Flip Pan and toss to coat shrimp cook for 2 minutes.

Add the stir fry sauce peppers and broccoli and cook for 2 minutes with lid closed add the remaining ingredients toss well and serve hot.

Total Cook Time: 15 minutes

NUTRITION FACTS

Serving Size: ¼ of a recipe

AMOUNT PER SERVING	% DAILY VALUE
Calories: 265	13%
Calories from Fat: 67	10%
Total Fat: 7g	11%
Saturated Fat: 1g	5%
Cholesterol: 151mg	50%
Sodium: 901mg	38%
Total Carbohydrates: 25g	8%
Fiber: 3g	12%
Sugars: 3g	
Protein: 18g	33%
Vitamin A:	28%
Vitamin C:	251%
Calcium:	5%
Iron:	46%

Josephine Cook's
Sweet and Sour Chicken

Serves 2

INGREDIENTS

1 20-ounce can pineapple chucks in juice,
    drain and reserve 2 tablespoons of juice
2 tablespoons vegetable oil, divided
1 large bell pepper, julienned
1 medium sweet onion, sliced thick
1 pound boneless, skinless, chicken breast, cut into 1-inch pieces
1 small can of water chestnuts, drained and rinsed
¾ cup sweet and sour sauce
¼ cup Thai sweet chili sauce with 1 tsp. minced fresh, garlic
1 tablespoon low sodium soy sauce
1 small carrot, julienned

DIRECTIONS

Heat the Jumbo Flip Pan on both sides for 3 minutes, on medium heat.

Open the lid. Add 1 tablespoon of the oil and add the onions, carrots and peppers.

NUTRITION FACTS

Serving Size: ½ of a recipe

AMOUNT PER SERVING	% DAILY VALUE
Calories: 138	7%
Calories from Fat: 23	3%
Total Fat: 3g	5%
Saturated Fat: 1g	5%
Cholesterol: 47mg	16%
Sodium: 235mg	10%
Total Carbohydrates: 11g	4%
Fiber: 4g	16%
Sugars: 0g	0%
Protein: 22g	40%
Vitamin A:	165%
Vitamin C:	54%
Calcium:	3%
Iron:	4%

Close the lid, cook for 4 minutes, then stir and cook for 4 minutes longer. This is for crisp veggies.

Remove the veggies.

Add the remaining oil and the chicken. Cook it for about 2 to 3 minutes with the

Lid open.

Close the lid for 3 minutes. Open the lid and check to see if the chicken is almost cooked.

Add the veggies, back in the pan, and stir.

Add the sweet and sour sauce, Thai chili sauce and soy sauce, stir.

Close the lid and cook and cook for 2 minutes.

Open the lid and add the water chestnuts, pineapple and the reserved pineapple juice.

Close the lid and cook 2 minutes.

Serve with Jasmine rice or whatever rice you like.

Linguine with Clam Sauce

A one pot Wonder offered by our friend Josephine Cook

INGREDIENTS

1 pound linguine pasta (or spaghetti)
1 cup clam juice
3 cups chicken broth
3 cloves garlic, sliced
2 tablespoons olive oil
1 10-oz. can of whole baby, clams,
   or 2 6.5-oz. cans of diced clams with the broth
½ teaspoon black pepper
¼ teaspoon hot pepper seeds (optional)
2 tablespoons fresh parsley

DIRECTIONS

If you are using an induction burner, the times are different, than another cooking surface. You would cook this recipe as follows:

Set induction burner to highest setting.

Place the linguine, chicken broth, clam juice, sliced garlic, olive oil, black pepper and if using hot pepper seeds, add now. If using fresh clams and parsley, add them in now, too. DO NOT ADD CANNED ONES IN YET.

Shut the lid and cook for 10 minutes. Open the lid, taste the pasta for your preference tenderness of the pasta. If you like it less al dente, cook a couple of minutes more.

If you used fresh clams, you are ready to eat.

NUTRITION FACTS

Serving Size: ¼ of a recipe

AMOUNT PER SERVING	% DAILY VALUE
Calories: 873	44%
Calories from Fat: 50	8%
Total Fat: 5g	8%
Saturated Fat: 1g	5%
Cholesterol: 0mg	0%
Sodium: 1901mg	79%
Total Carbohydrates: 84g	28%
Fiber: 4g	16%
Sugars: 4g	
Protein: 23g	42%
Vitamin A:	0%
Vitamin C:	0%
Calcium:	0%
Iron:	33%

If using canned clams, add them now, with the fresh parsley. Cook for another 1 to 2 minutes. Do not overcook the clams, they will get tough.

If using another cooking surface, I used a glass top. You would cook this recipe as follows:

Set the temperature at medium high. Place the chicken broth, clam juice in the pan. Shut the lid and bring to a boil.

Add the linguine, chicken broth, clam juice, sliced garlic, olive oil, black pepper and hot pepper seed, if using.

Cook for 10 minutes. Open the lid and check for tenderness. If you like it cooked more, shut the lid and cook for 1 to 2 minutes.

Open the lid, add the clams and parsley. Cook for 1 to 2 minutes. Do not overcook the clams, as they will be tough.

The chicken broth and the clam juice are quite flavorful, so taste to see if you want to add any salt.

TIP: you can use fresh little neck or cherrystone clams for this recipe. Make sure you wash them and check that they are all closed.

Remember if you are using angel hair, the cooking time would be less.

Lobster Macaroni and Cheese

INGREDIENTS

6½ pounds live Maine lobster

sea salt, to taste

½ pound of dry pasta

1 cup heavy cream

¼ cup whipped cream cheese

¼ cup white Vermont cheddar, shredded

¼ cup Fontina cheese, shredded

¼ cup parmesan, shredded

fresh ground black pepper

pinch of nutmeg

¼ cup panko crumbs

1 tablespoon butter

DIRECTIONS

Fill jumbo Flip Pan half way with water add sea salt a tablespoon at a time till the water taste a little salty—like the ocean. Close Flip Pan and bring to a boil.

Add the lobster head first. Close Flip Pan and set timer. 8 minutes for 1lb, up to 12 minutes for 1 ½ pounder.

When cook time is complete, remove the lobster from boiling water and set aside to clean.

Add the dry pasta to the lobster water and cook according to package directions.

Drain the pasta, reserving ¼ cup of cooking liquid.

Add the ¼ cup of cooking liquid to the Flip Pan and stir in the cream cheese over medium heat till smooth. Add the cream and bring to a simmer.

Remove the Flip Pan from the burner and stir in the 3 cheeses, stir till smooth and all cheese dissolved.

Remove the meat from the claws and tail of the lobster. Set aside.

NUTRITION FACTS

Serving Size: ¼ of a recipe

AMOUNT PER SERVING	% DAILY VALUE
Calories: 1261	63%
Calories from Fat: 334	50%
Total Fat: 38g	58%
Saturated Fat: 12g	60%
Cholesterol: 603mg	201%
Sodium: 1349mg	56%
Total Carbohydrates: 59g	20%
Fiber: 2g	8%
Sugars: 2g	
Protein: 159g	289%
Vitamin A:	22%
Vitamin C:	25%
Calcium:	35%
Iron:	59%

Melt the butter and toss with panko. Remove the lid from the Flip Pan and place over medium heat and toast the panko and butter till golden brown.

Toss the pasta with the cheese sauce season with pepper and nutmeg, then mix in lobster chunks. Sprinkle with golden brown crumbs.

Cook time 30 minutes

Jill Allmandinger Moyer's Sausage and Potatoes

Serves 4

INGREDIENTS

1 pound ground Italian sausage

½ sweet onion

1 pound small potatoes, quartered

2 cloves of garlic, minced

1 pint cherry tomatoes, halved

1 tablespoon fresh rosemary, chopped

1 tablespoon fresh basil, chopped

salt and pepper, to taste

garlic and herb basting oil

DIRECTIONS

Preheat pan on deep side

Cook sausage in the Flip Pan with medium-high heat; add onions half way through continue cooking. Remove mixture.

Add potatoes and basting oil, salt and pepper, stirring often till brown

Cooking approximately 10 minutes depending on size of the potatoes (mine were pre-cooked). Return sausage onion mixture. Add tomatoes, rosemary and basil—cook another 5 minutes.

NUTRITION FACTS

Serving Size: ¼ of a recipe

AMOUNT PER SERVING	% DAILY VALUE
Calories: 458	23%
Calories from Fat: 304	46%
Total Fat: 34g	52%
Saturated Fat: 13g	65%
Cholesterol: 64mg	21%
Sodium: 840mg	35%
Total Carbohydrates: 20g	7%
Fiber: 2g	8%
Sugars: 0g	0%
Protein: 19g	35%
Vitamin A:	3%
Vitamin C:	36%
Calcium:	0%
Iron:	12%

One Pot Pasta Caprese

INGREDIENTS

4 cups water

1 pound angel hair pasta

2 cloves garlic, sliced

1 cup petite diced or 1 pint grape tomato, sliced

1 cup fresh baby spinach

8 leaves basil

½ cup mini mozzarella balls or fresh mozzarella

1 teaspoon olive oil

2 tablespoons pesto

1 teaspoon sea salt

DIRECTIONS

Bring the water to boil in the Flip Pan.

Add the remaining ingredients, stir, and lower heat to medium.

Cover and cook for 6 minutes.

Stir and serve.

NUTRITION FACTS

Serving Size: ¼ of a recipe

AMOUNT PER SERVING	% DAILY VALUE
Calories: 449	22%
Calories from Fat: 30	4%
Total Fat: 3g	5%
Saturated Fat: 0g	0%
Cholesterol: 0mg	0%
Sodium: 605mg	25%
Total Carbohydrates: 85g	28%
Fiber: 5g	20%
Sugars: 4g	
Protein: 16g	29%
Vitamin A:	8%
Vitamin C:	16%
Calcium:	0%
Iron:	21%

Stuffed Cabbage

Michael Caldwell one of our key members to the Flip Pan Group on Facebook. Michael is posting and encouraging others constantly.

INGREDIENTS

1 large firm head of cabbage

1 large onion, diced

1 12-ounce package of bacon

1 pack meatloaf mix, between one and 1½ pounds.

1 package three-quarters of a pound to 1-pound of ground beef

1 package boil in the bag white rice, prepare as directed on the box, for only six minutes, not 10, then set aside to cool

1 32-ounce can tomato, sauce

1 32-ounce jar sauerkraut

Salt and pepper

DIRECTIONS

Preheat pan on both sides.

With a paring knife cut around and remove core from cabbage head. Place cabbage in large pot of water and bring to a simmering boil for 10 to 15 minutes. Peel off leaves and place in a large bowl or glass baking dish. Let cool. In the Flip Pan, on medium high heat, render the fat from the bacon. Do not crisp or brown. Remove from pan to paper towels to drain. Season chopped onion with salt and pepper and sauté in the bacon fat. When onions are translucent remove pan from heat to cool. In a large bowl add the meat loaf mix and ground beef, season with salt and pepper, and

NUTRITION FACTS

Serving Size: ⅙ of a recipe

AMOUNT PER SERVING	% DAILY VALUE
Calories: 5	0%
Calories from Fat: 0	0%
Total Fat: 0g	0%
Saturated Fat: 0g	0%
Cholesterol: 0mg	0%
Sodium: 32mg	1%
Total Carbohydrates: 1g	0%
Fiber: 0g	0%
Sugars: 0g	0%
Protein: 0g	0%
Vitamin A:	1%
Vitamin C:	5%
Calcium:	0%
Iron:	0%

cooled onions and cooled rice. Mix until thoroughly combined. Using a sharp paring knife slice the thick rib off of each leaf. Lay one leaf at a time on your hand and an appropriate amount of meat mixture depending on the size of the leaf. With the meat oval-shaped lay it on the leaf in the same direction as the rib. Fold the bottom of the leaf where you slice the rib off over the bottom of the meat. Roll one side of leaf over the meat and then roll the other side over the meat. Using your index finger take the top of the leaf into the roll. Set aside until all leaves are rolled. Use any remaining meat to make small meatballs about the size of a tennis ball or less set aside. Take the cabbage head that was left after the leaves are peeled and sliced in the corners. Put the Flip Pan back on the burner on medium low heat. Using half the jar of sauerkraut cover the bottom of the pan. Lay in as many cabbage rolls that will fit. Cover that layer with two thirds of the bacon and then add on top of that the remaining cabbage rolls, meatballs, and the quartered cabbage. Layer on the remaining bacon and the other half of the jar of sauerkraut. Add the can of tomato sauce and approximately ½ to ⅔ of a can of water. Close the pan, Cook for approximately 90 minutes, then turn off the heat and let sit for another 30 minutes. Open the lid and take one of the meatballs and slice it in half to make sure they are cooked through. You are now done.

Jumbo Flip Pan
Proteins

Braised Short Ribs

This tender meat will comfort your heart and stomach . . .

INGREDIENTS

1 tablespoon olive oil

4–6 pounds beef short ribs

½ teaspoon salt

2 medium onions, chopped

4 gloves garlic, minced

1 cup red wine

1 28-ounce can whole tomato, with juice

2 tablespoons Worcestershire Sauce

1 sprig rosemary

1 cup frozen pearl onion

1 pound baby carrots

DIRECTIONS

Preheat oven to 350 degrees

Place the Flip Pan onto stove and set to medium high heat.

Let heat for 2 minutes then add in the oil and heat 2 minutes longer.

Pat the ribs with paper towels to remove the moisture. Season both sides with salt.

When the oil and pot are hot, carefully add the ribs and sear all sides with no lid.

Add all the remaining ingredients and stir.

Close Flip Pan and place in the oven. Set timer for 3 hours

At the end of 3 hours ribs will be tender. Carefully remove the ribs to a platter.

Place the Flip Pan back on the stove and remove the rosemary sprig.

Skim fat from sauce and reduce the cooking liquid by half approximately 5 minutes.

Cook Time: 2 hours

NUTRITION FACTS

Serving Size: ⅙ of a recipe

AMOUNT PER SERVING	% DAILY VALUE
Calories: 564	28%
Calories from Fat: 198	30%
Total Fat: 25g	38%
Saturated Fat: 7g	35%
Cholesterol: 196mg	65%
Sodium: 1730mg	72%
Total Carbohydrates: 13g	4%
Fiber: 2g	8%
Sugars: 4g	
Protein: 74g	135%
Vitamin A:	294%
Vitamin C:	15%
Calcium:	2%
Iron:	36%

Beer Steamed Clams

Serves 4

These are the most incredible clams I have ever eaten!

NGREDIENTS

1 12-ounce bottle pale lager
5 pounds hard-shell clams (such as littlenecks), scrubbed
1 teaspoon Cajun seasoning
2 tablespoons melted butter
1 tablespoon fresh chopped parsley
lemon halves, for serving

DIRECTIONS

Bring beer to a boil in Jumbo Flip Pan with seasoning and lemon
Close lid will take about 2 minutes.

Add clams. Close Flip Pan, reduce heat to medium, and steam
clams until they open, 6–8 minutes.

Pour melted butter through the infuser and shake to coat the
clams.

Sprinkle with fresh parsley

NUTRITION FACTS

Serving Size: ¼ of a recipe

AMOUNT PER SERVING	% DAILY VALUE
Calories: 610	31%
Calories from Fat: 50	8%
Total Fat: 6g	9%
Saturated Fat: 0g	0%
Cholesterol: 458mg	153%
Sodium: 2971mg	124%
Total Carbohydrates: 24g	8%
Fiber: 0g	0%
Sugars: 0g	0%
Protein: 89g	162%
Vitamin A:	4%
Vitamin C:	12%
Calcium:	1%
Iron:	22%

Chicken Cacciatore

Delicious melt in your mouth flavor filled chicken in under a half an hour

INGREDIENTS

2 bone-in thighs skin removed

2 bone-in breasts skin removed

Salt and pepper

1 tablespoon olive oil

cup of chicken stock

small onion, diced

small pepper, diced

2 cloves garlic

1 14.5-ounce can of petite diced tomato

1 tablespoon capers

DIRECTIONS

Let chicken parts sit at room temperature for at least 20 minutes.

Remove all excess moisture from the chicken, rub with oil and season with salt and pepper.

Place Flip Pan on medium high heat top and bottom for a couple of minutes.

Brown the chicken on both sides till golden brown with lid open.

Add the remaining ingredients and cook for 20 minutes with lid closed.

NUTRITION FACTS

Serving Size: ¼ of a recipe

AMOUNT PER SERVING	% DAILY VALUE
Calories: 16	1%
Calories from Fat: 3	0%
Total Fat: 0g	0%
Saturated Fat: 0g	0%
Cholesterol: 0mg	0%
Sodium: 181mg	8%
Total Carbohydrates: 2g	1%
Fiber: 0g	0%
Sugars: 0g	0%
Protein: 2g	4%
Vitamin A:	0%
Vitamin C:	5%
Calcium:	0%
Iron:	0%

Broasted Chicken

Best Fried Chicken Ever!

INGREDIENTS

8 pieces chicken, bone in
½ cup salt
2 quarts water
2 cups all-purpose flour
1 teaspoon salt
1 teaspoon pepper
1 teaspoon poultry seasoning
1 teaspoon Fine Herbs
1 teaspoon Accent Seasoning
1 quart oil or shortening

DIRECTIONS

Place chicken parts in 2 quarts of water with ½ cup of salt dissolved in it. Brine for 6 hours.

Mix the flour with the seasonings in a large bowl.

Fill Jumbo Flip Pan ⅓ way with oil or shortening, bring oil to 350 degrees.

Take each piece of the chicken from the brine right into the flour. Shake off extra and place in the oil. Repeat with the remaining pieces. Cook chicken on each side with lid open till golden brown, approximately 5 minutes per side. Seal the Flip Pan and cook for 7 minutes under pressure. Drain on paper towels.

NUTRITION FACTS

Serving Size: 2 pieces

AMOUNT PER SERVING	% DAILY VALUE
Calories: 350	
Calories from Fat: 171	
Total Fat: 19g	29%
Saturated Fat: 3g	15%
Cholesterol: 105mg	35%
Sodium: 1270mg	53%
Total Carbohydrates: 18g	6%
Fiber: 1g	4%
Sugars: 0g	0%
Protein: 27g	
Vitamin A:	2%
Vitamin C:	4%
Calcium:	4%
Iron:	10%

Clam Bake

Serves 4

INGREDIENTS

1 medium sweet onion, quartered

1 tablespoon olive oil

2 cups water

1 pound small potatoes (red or white)

½ tablespoon kosher salt

½ tablespoon freshly ground black pepper

2 1½-pound lobsters

½ cup good dry white wine

2 dozens littleneck clams, scrubbed

1 pound large shrimp, in the shell

1 lemon, halved

DIRECTIONS

Preheat Flip Pan over medium high heat for two minutes.

Add the onion and the oil and cook for 3 minutes with lid closed.

Add the water and potatoes and seasoning and close lid and bring to a boil.

Add the lobsters head down into Flip Pan, close the lid and set timer for 8 minutes.

If you have the new infuser pan add the wine thru the infuser hole.

Add the remaining ingredients and cook for 3 minutes longer with lid closed.

Serve with lemon and drawn butter.

NUTRITION FACTS

Serving Size: ¼ of a recipe

AMOUNT PER SERVING	% DAILY VALUE
Calories: 177	9%
Calories from Fat: 34	5%
Total Fat: 4g	6%
Saturated Fat: 1g	5%
Cholesterol: 151mg	50%
Sodium: 1948mg	81%
Total Carbohydrates: 20g	7%
Fiber: 2g	8%
Sugars: 2g	
Protein: 15g	27%
Vitamin A:	0%
Vitamin C:	23%
Calcium:	3%
Iron:	6%

Corned Beef and Cabbage

INGREDIENTS

1 corned beef brisket (2 to 2 ½ pounds) with seasoning packet
8 small red bliss potatoes
6 large carrots, peeled and cut into 2 inch pieces
1 large sweet onion, quartered
1 cabbage, quartered
1 12-ounce bottle dark beer
1 cup beef stock
1 sprig thyme

DIRECTIONS

With a sharp knife score the fat on corned beef.

Preheat oven to 350 degrees.

Place the jumbo Flip Pan onto burner on medium high.

Place the corned beef in pan fat side down and sear well.

Flip the corned beef over and sear 4 more minutes.

Add all ingredients into the Flip Pan, close the lid and bring to a boil approximately 10 minutes.

Place the closed Flip Pan in preheated oven for 5 hours.

Remove all the meat and veggies to a platter to keep warm, discard the sprig of thyme, and place Flip Pan back on medium high burner. Defat. Plus reduce the cooking liquid by half.

Pour cooking liquid over meat and veggies and serve warm.

NUTRITION FACTS

Serving Size: ⅙ of a recipe

AMOUNT PER SERVING	% DAILY VALUE
Calories: 179	9%
Calories from Fat: 11	2%
Total Fat: 2g	3%
Saturated Fat: 0g	0%
Cholesterol: 12mg	4%
Sodium: 127mg	5%
Total Carbohydrates: 34g	11%
Fiber: 5g	20%
Sugars: 2g	
Protein: 8g	15%
Vitamin A:	330%
Vitamin C:	28%
Calcium:	3%
Iron:	5%

Italian Pot Roast

Serves 4

INGREDIENTS

2 tablespoons extra-virgin olive oil
1 chuck roast (3–4 pounds)
1 teaspoon salt
½ teaspoon freshly ground pepper
¼ cup dry red wine
1 cup beef stock
1 medium onion, sliced
3 garlic cloves, sliced
1 bell pepper, sliced
1 teaspoon garlic powder
1 teaspoon Italian herb seasoning
5 pepperoncini peppers
1 bay leaf
1 bottle (28 ounces) favorite pasta sauce
favorite pasta, cooked

NUTRITION FACTS

Serving Size: ¼ of a recipe

AMOUNT PER SERVING	% DAILY VALUE
Calories: 117	6%
Calories from Fat: 77	12%
Total Fat: 9g	14%
Saturated Fat: 2g	10%
Cholesterol: 18mg	6%
Sodium: 733mg	31%
Total Carbohydrates: 3g	1%
Fiber: 0g	0%
Sugars: 0g	0%
Protein: 7g	13%
Vitamin A:	0%
Vitamin C:	5%
Calcium:	0%
Iron:	4%

DIRECTIONS

Preheat oven to 350 degrees

Place Jumbo Flip Pan on medium high heat add oil and let heat for 2 minutes.

Season the roast with salt and pepper.

Add the chuck roast to the Flip Pan and sear for 3 minutes on each side.

Add the wine and stock to the Flip Pan and bring to a boil with lid closed.

Add remaining ingredients except for pasta.

Close the lid and set in the preheated oven and cook for 2 hours or tender.

When cooking is complete discard bay leaf and serve over pasta.

Cook Time 2½ hours

Jeanine Shuta Suhanick's Sirloin Tip Roast with Potatoes and Carrots

Serves 6

INGREDIENTS

4 pounds sirloin tip roast

3 tablespoons olive oil

1 large clove garlic, peeled and minced

2 teaspoons fresh parsley, chopped

½ teaspoon thyme leaves, chopped

½ cup red wine

½ cup apple juice

1 package beefy onion soup mix

1 good quality beef bouillon cube

2 caps of gravy master

½ jar chili sauce or ketchup

1 teaspoon pepper

1 tablespoon parsley

3 cut up potatoes, about 1 inch

4 cut up carrots, about 1 inch

NUTRITION FACTS

Serving Size: ⅙ of a recipe

AMOUNT PER SERVING	% DAILY VALUE
Calories: 73	4%
Calories from Fat: 2	0%
Total Fat: 0g	0%
Saturated Fat: 0g	0%
Cholesterol: 0mg	0%
Sodium: 211mg	9%
Total Carbohydrates: 16g	5%
Fiber: 2g	8%
Sugars: 2g	
Protein: 2g	4%
Vitamin A:	220%
Vitamin C:	14%
Calcium:	2%
Iron:	1%

DIRECTIONS

Season the roast and let rest.

Combine in a bowl all the ingredients except potatoes and carrots.

Heat the pan on both sides.

Open and put the oil in, sear the roast on all sides. Brown on all sides in the Jumbo Flip Pan.

Add all the ingredients.

Close the lid. Cook the roast 15 minutes per pound for 1 hour. Add the potatoes and carrots and cook 15 more minutes, with the roast, until fork tender.

Tender Meatballs Stuffed with Mozzarella Cheese

Serves 6

Great as an appetizer or over pasta!

INGREDIENTS

1½ cups fresh bread crumbs, torn

2 cups heavy cream

2 cups beef stock

1 pound ground chuck

½ pound ground pork

½ pound ground veal (optional)

3 garlic cloves, grated

1 small onion, grated

¾ cup Romano cheese, grated

1 teaspoon salt

½ teaspoon freshly ground pepper

¼ cup parsley, chopped fine

2 large eggs, beaten

8 ounces smoked mozzarella, diced into ½ inch cubes

4 cups homemade or bottled pasta sauces

NUTRITION FACTS

Serving Size: ⅙ of a recipe

AMOUNT PER SERVING	% DAILY VALUE
Calories: 619	31%
Calories from Fat: 424	64%
Total Fat: 50g	77%
Saturated Fat: 24g	120%
Cholesterol: 219mg	73%
Sodium: 1280mg	53%
Total Carbohydrates: 21g	7%
Fiber: 1g	4%
Sugars: 2g	
Protein: 20g	36%
Vitamin A:	23%
Vitamin C:	3%
Calcium:	16%
Iron:	15%

DIRECTIONS

In a bowl soak the bread crumbs in heavy cream

Pour Stock into Flip Pan and bring to a boil.

Add to the bread crumb mixture remaining ingredients except for the mozzarella and sauce.

Gently incorporate the ingredients and form into 2 inch balls

Press a piece of mozzarella into the center of each meatball and re roll to make round again.

Gently drop the meatballs into the hot stock in the Flip Pan.

Cook for 10 minutes with lid closed.

Strain off the stock and add cups of pasta sauce. Close and heat 5 minutes longer.

Serve with heated pasta sauce

Michael Caldwell's Carmella's Vinegar Garlic Chicken Thighs

The color of the chicken is wonderful. The chicken is so flavorful and delicious. The garlic slices are as soft as butter. You taste the vinegar and garlic, but their flavor is now soft and rich.

INGREDIENTS

4 chicken thighs, bone-in, with skin
1 whole garlic clove
½ cup red wine vinegar, divided
1½ cups chicken broth
extra virgin olive oil
salt and pepper

DIRECTIONS

Preheat pan on medium heat.

Add ¼ cup Extra Virgin Olive Oil to pan.

Season thighs with salt and pepper on both sides.

Add chicken to pan, close lid, brown on both sides. Approximately 3–4 minutes each side.

Remove chicken from pan.

Reduce heat to low.

NUTRITION FACTS

Serving Size: ¼ of a recipe

AMOUNT PER SERVING	% DAILY VALUE
Calories: 335	17%
Calories from Fat: 84	13%
Total Fat: 9g	14%
Saturated Fat: 3g	15%
Cholesterol: 44mg	15%
Sodium: 789mg	33%
Total Carbohydrates: 1g	0%
Fiber: 0g	0%
Sugars: 0g	0%
Protein: 2g	4%
Vitamin A:	2%
Vitamin C:	0%
Calcium:	1%
Iron:	3%

Season garlic with salt and pepper, add to pan, sauté until garlic starts to soften and change color. I did this with the pan open, because if you burn the garlic the dish is ruined.

At this point, add ¼ cup vinegar, stir and close lid for 8 minutes, checking after 4 minutes.

After 8 minutes, open pan and add chicken broth, stir, return chicken to pan.

Increase heat to medium low, close lid.

Cook for 20 minutes, open pan, turn chicken and add remaining vinegar.

Close lid and cook another 20 minutes.

Open lid and raise heat to medium and reduce liquid by half, turning chicken several times.

When serving, pour some of pan sauce and garlic over each piece.

Pot Roast

Serves 4

INGREDIENTS

3–4 lbs. chuck roast

flour, for dusting roast

½ teaspoon salt

½ teaspoon freshly ground pepper

2 tablespoons vegetable oil

2 medium onions, peeled and sliced

3 cups beef broth, divided

1 bay leaf

1 sprig rosemary

3 cloves garlic, minced

¼ cup of red wine

3 carrots, peeled, cut into 3-inch pieces

2 stalks celery, diced small

8 baby red potatoes

1 tablespoon tomato paste

2 tablespoons butter

NUTRITION FACTS

Serving Size: ¼ of a recipe

AMOUNT PER SERVING	% DAILY VALUE
Calories: 329	16%
Calories from Fat: 50	8%
Total Fat: 6g	9%
Saturated Fat: 0g	0%
Cholesterol: 15mg	5%
Sodium: 1735mg	72%
Total Carbohydrates: 56g	19%
Fiber: 9g	36%
Sugars: 0g	0%
Protein: 13g	24%
Vitamin A:	252%
Vitamin C:	116%
Calcium:	2%
Iron:	19%

DIRECTIONS

With the Flip Pan open set the burner to medium high to brown add the oil let heat a minute.

Rub roast with flour and salt and pepper.

Place the roast in the Flip Pan and brown both sides at least 3 minutes per side.

Add the onions, broth, bay leaf, rosemary garlic and wine to the pan.

Continued >>

Close the lid, Set a timer for 60 minutes.

When cooking cycle is complete add the remaining ingredients but the butter.

Secure the lid, and set timer for 30 minutes longer. Add remaining stock at this point

When cook time is complete, remove roast and vegetables to a platter, discard the bay leaf and rosemary.

With the lid open over a medium high heat reduce the liquid by half, when the sauce is starting to thicken, whisk in the butter one tablespoon at a time.

Pour sauce over meat and serve hot.

Roasted Turkey

I adore turkey and this is how I prepare my turkey, I love using the Jumbo Flip Pan to roast, then make my pan gravy in the lid after

INGREDIENTS

1 turkey, approximately 15 pounds

juice of a lemon

salt and pepper

olive oil or melted butter

½ yellow onion, peeled and quartered

tops and bottoms of a bunch of celery

2 tablespoons of each of the following fresh herbs:

    parsley

    thyme

    rosemary

    sage

DIRECTIONS

Preheat oven to 350 degrees

Remove the giblets and neck from the inside of the turkey reserve

Rinse turkey and pat dry.

Let turkey rest at room temperature for at least ½ hour before roasting.

Place roasting rack in Jumbo Flip Pan bottom

Stuff the cavity of the turkey with the onion celery and herbs.

Truss the turkey with butchers twine.

NUTRITION FACTS

Serving Size: ⅛ of a recipe

AMOUNT PER SERVING	% DAILY VALUE
Calories: 3	0%
Calories from Fat: 0	0%
Total Fat: 0g	0%
Saturated Fat: 0g	0%
Cholesterol: 0mg	0%
Sodium: 1mg	0%
Total Carbohydrates: 1g	0%
Fiber: 0g	0%
Sugars: 0g	0%
Protein: 0g	0%
Vitamin A:	0%
Vitamin C:	6%
Calcium:	0%
Iron:	0%

Continued >>

Rub the turkey exterior really well with butter or olive oil, then rub with salt and pepper.

Place the turkey in the oven—consider 12–13 minutes per pound. So approximately 2 ½ hours.

I make turkey stock by cooking the neck and giblets in 4 cups of chicken stock, the last half hour I baste by pouring stock over breast portion every 10 minutes.

Remove the turkey and rack from the Jumbo Flip Pan. Let rest.

Pour the liquid from pan to a measuring cup for defatting.

For gravy I take 2 tablespoons of butter and 2 tablespoons of gravy flour and melt together well, add in the pan drippings and turkey stock to measure 2 ups of liquid. Whisk well and bring to a simmer.

Tender Turkey Meatballs

These light meatballs are almost like dumplings when cooked in your Jumbo Flip Pan

INGREDIENTS

1 tablespoon olive oil

1 teaspoon salt

½ teaspoon freshly ground black pepper

1 small onion, minced

2 garlic cloves, minced

1 pound ground turkey

½ cup Italian bread crumbs

1 can (14 ounces) diced tomato

1 large egg, beaten

¼ cup Parmesan cheese, grated

2 tablespoons parsley, chopped

2 cups chicken stock

DIRECTIONS

Pre heat jumbo Flip Pan over medium heat for 2 minutes, add the oil and let heat 2 minutes longer.

Add the onions and garlic to the Flip Pan close lid and cook for 5 minutes.

Transfer the onion mixture to a bowl and let cool.

In a separate bowl, combine the breadcrumbs, egg, cheese, parsley, salt and pepper.

Add the onion mixture and turkey to the bowl and mix well using your hands.

Form the turkey mixture into golf ball sized meatballs.

Place the tomatoes and stock into the jumbo Flip Pan; secure lid.

Set timer for 5 minutes

Add the meatballs to the jumbo Flip Pan.

Close the lid and set timer for 20 minutes.

Drain off remaining stock and pour in the pasta sauce to the Flip Pan, stir and let the sauce heat through. Approx. 10 minutes.

Serve hot over pasta.

NUTRITION FACTS

Serving Size: ¼ of a recipe

AMOUNT PER SERVING	% DAILY VALUE
Calories: 245	12%
Calories from Fat: 64	10%
Total Fat: 8g	12%
Saturated Fat: 2g	10%
Cholesterol: 113mg	38%
Sodium: 537mg	22%
Total Carbohydrates: 2g	1%
Fiber: 0g	0%
Sugars: 0g	0%
Protein: 23g	42%
Vitamin A:	1%
Vitamin C:	5%
Calcium:	9%
Iron:	3%

Original Flip Pan
Side Dishes

Balsamic Glazed Brussel Sprouts

INGREDIENTS

10 ounces brussels sprouts
1 teaspoon salt
1 teaspoon sugar
½ teaspoon pepper
1 tablespoon unsalted butter
1 tablespoon olive oil
1 small red onion, thinly sliced lengthwise
2 tablespoons balsamic vinegar reduction
pomegranate seeds

DIRECTIONS

Place Flip Pan on medium heat and add a cup of water

Bring water to a boil and add salt and sugar.

Trim outer leaves and stems from brussel sprouts, and discard.

Meanwhile, prepare an ice-water bath.

Add brussel sprouts to boiling water, and cook until tender but still bright green, about 4 minutes.

Remove from heat, drain, and plunge into ice-water bath to cool. Drain well, and cut in fourths.

Place the Flip Pan back onto stove on medium high.

Let heat for 2 minutes then add in ½ tablespoon of butter and ½ tablespoon oil.

Add brussels sprouts, and cook with lid closed flipping occasionally, until they are brown and crisp on the edges, about 3 minutes.
Season to taste with salt and pepper, and transfer to a large bowl. Cover with aluminum foil to keep warm.

Add remaining ½ tablespoon each butter and oil to the pan.

Add onions, and cook with lid closed until tender, about 3 to 4 minutes.

Mix the onions with brussel sprouts, drizzle with Balsamic reduction and sprinkle with pomegranate seeds.

NUTRITION FACTS

Serving Size: ¼ of a recipe

AMOUNT PER SERVING	% DAILY VALUE
Calories: 96	5%
Calories from Fat: 55	8%
Total Fat: 6g	9%
Saturated Fat: 1g	5%
Cholesterol: 8mg	3%
Sodium: 634mg	26%
Total Carbohydrates: 7g	2%
Fiber: 3g	12%
Sugars: 3g	
Protein: 3g	5%
Vitamin A:	7%
Vitamin C:	66%
Calcium:	2%
Iron:	2%

Grilled Vegetable Tortellini Primavera Serves 4

INGREDIENTS

3 medium zucchini and/or yellow squash, cut into rounds

½ cup broccoli flowerets

1 red onion, sliced into ½-inch rounds

4 mushroom caps, sliced

1 pint cherry or grape tomatoes, halved

1 red bell pepper, cut into strips

¼ cup of extra virgin olive oil

4 cloves of garlic, minced

1 cup white wine

½ cup chicken broth

¾ cup good quality Parmesan cheese, grated

¼ cup fresh basil, chopped

¼ cup fresh parsley, chopped

salt and fresh ground pepper, to taste

1 pound tortellini, stuffed with pesto

NUTRITION FACTS

Serving Size: ¼ of a recipe

AMOUNT PER SERVING	% DAILY VALUE
Calories: 743	37%
Calories from Fat: 193	29%
Total Fat: 25g	38%
Saturated Fat: 7g	35%
Cholesterol: 23mg	8%
Sodium: 1223mg	51%
Total Carbohydrates: 98g	33%
Fiber: 20g	80%
Sugars: 0g	0%
Protein: 22g	40%
Vitamin A:	18%
Vitamin C:	81%
Calcium:	29%
Iron:	2%

DIRECTIONS

Preheat the Flip Pan on medium heat top and bottom.

Toss all the vegetables in the olive oil.

Add the squash first to the grill pan, grill 2 minutes per side with lid open.

Remove to a platter, add the purple onion and broccoli cook for 2 minutes per side with lid closed, remove the broccoli and add the pepper strip to the pan and cook for 3 minutes with the lid open.

Add all the remaining ingredients to the pan, stir well close lid and cook for 8 minutes over medium heat.

Cherie Bream Estok's
Sweet Potatoes with Pineapple

Serves 4

INGREDIENTS

2 large sweet potatoes, peeled and chopped into 2-inch chunks
4 tablespoons butter
½ cup water
¼ cup brown sugar
¼ cup chopped pineapple

DIRECTIONS

Preheat the Flip Pan, 3–4 minutes on each side. After heating, add the first four ingredients into the pan.

Cook for approximately 10 minutes with the lid down on medium heat. Test to see if the potatoes are soft by gently putting a fork into the middle of one of the sweet potato chunks. When they are soft, add ¼ cup of freshly cut (or canned) pineapple chunks and heat for another 3–4 minutes and serve.

NUTRITION FACTS

Serving Size: ¼ of a recipe

AMOUNT PER SERVING	% DAILY VALUE
Calories: 169	8%
Calories from Fat: 0	0%
Total Fat: 0g	0%
Saturated Fat: 0g	0%
Cholesterol: 0mg	0%
Sodium: 43mg	2%
Total Carbohydrates: 44g	15%
Fiber: 4g	16%
Sugars: 19g	
Protein: 2g	4%
Vitamin A:	421%
Vitamin C:	29%
Calcium:	2%
Iron:	2%

Copper Carrots

INGREDIENTS

2 cups chicken stock

½ teaspoon sugar

1 pound peeled carrots, diagonally cut (or baby carrots)

2 tablespoons butter

2 tablespoons honey

1 tablespoon lemon juice

freshly ground black pepper

¼ cup flat-leaf parsley, chopped

DIRECTIONS

Place Flip Pan on a medium high burner.

Add 2 cups stock and bring to a boil about 3 minutes.

Add sugar and then carrots and cook until tender, 5 to 6 minutes.

Drain the carrots and add back to pan with butter, honey and lemon juice.

Cook until a glaze coats the carrots, 5 minutes.

Season with salt and pepper and garnish with parsley.

NUTRITION FACTS

Serving Size: ½ of a recipe

AMOUNT PER SERVING	% DAILY VALUE
Calories: 262	13%
Calories from Fat: 110	16%
Total Fat: 13g	20%
Saturated Fat: 0g	0%
Cholesterol: 30mg	10%
Sodium: 853mg	36%
Total Carbohydrates: 33g	11%
Fiber: 4g	16%
Sugars: 17g	
Protein: 6g	11%
Vitamin A:	668%
Vitamin C:	16%
Calcium:	4%
Iron:	0%

Grilled German Potato Salad

Serves 4

INGREDIENTS

1 ½ pounds small bliss, potatoes

1 ½ teaspoons table, salt

¼ teaspoon ground black pepper

4 slices bacon, cut crosswise into ¼-inch strips

1 small sweet onion, diced

1 teaspoon mustard powder

3 tablespoons apple cider vinegar

1 teaspoon salt

1 teaspoon sugar

½ teaspoon ground black pepper

1 rib celery, chopped fine (about ¼ cup)

2 tablespoons fresh parsley leaves, minced

DIRECTIONS

Place the potatoes, bacon salt and pepper in Flip Pan, grill side facing up. Over medium heat cook till potatoes are tender (about 10 minutes).

Add the vinegar mustard powder salt, sugar and pepper. Cook for 2 minutes longer.

Pour into a bowl and add remaining ingredients. Serve warm.

NUTRITION FACTS

Serving Size: ¼ of a recipe

AMOUNT PER SERVING	% DAILY VALUE
Calories: 147	7%
Calories from Fat: 30	4%
Total Fat: 3g	5%
Saturated Fat: 1g	5%
Cholesterol: 5mg	2%
Sodium: 152mg	6%
Total Carbohydrates: 26g	9%
Fiber: 3g	12%
Sugars: 2g	
Protein: 5g	9%
Vitamin A:	0%
Vitamin C:	36%
Calcium:	6%
Iron:	2%

Easy Macaroni and Cheese

INGREDIENTS

3 cups elbow macaroni

3 cups chicken stock

pinch salt and fresh ground pepper

1 cup heavy cream

½ cup mozzarella, shredded

½ cup Parmesan cheese, grated

1 cup cheddar cheese, shredded

DIRECTIONS

Place the chicken stock in the Flip Pan and bring to a boil over medium high heat.

Add the elbows to the stock and close the Flip Pan and set timer for 8 minutes.

When the timer goes off, open the lid and add the cream.

When cream starts to bubble (approximately 2 minutes.)

Stir in the cheeses and continue to stir till cheese is melted about 2 minutes.

Close the lid and cook for 2 additional minutes per side.

When complete invert onto a platter to see the golden brown goodness.

NUTRITION FACTS

Serving Size: ⅙ of a recipe

AMOUNT PER SERVING	% DAILY VALUE
Calories: 296	15%
Calories from Fat: 168	25%
Total Fat: 20g	31%
Saturated Fat: 10g	50%
Cholesterol: 63mg	21%
Sodium: 520mg	22%
Total Carbohydrates: 20g	7%
Fiber: 3g	12%
Sugars: 0g	0%
Protein: 11g	20%
Vitamin A:	11%
Vitamin C:	0%
Calcium:	12%
Iron:	0%

Quinoa Tabbouleh

Healthy delicious Side dish

INGREDIENTS

1 cup quinoa, rinsed
2½ cups water
1 teaspoon salt
1 cup grape tomatoes, diced
1 tablespoon flat leaf parsley, finely chopped
1 tablespoon mint, finely chopped
6 green onions, finely sliced
6 tablespoons extra-virgin olive oil
2 tablespoons fresh lemon juice

DIRECTIONS

Place the water in the Flip Pan and bring to a boil over medium heat.

Add the rinsed quinoa and salt. Stir close lid and cook for 15 minutes over medium.

Transfer the quinoa to a bowl and let cool.

Add remaining ingredients to the bowl, stir and serve

NUTRITION FACTS

Serving Size: ¼ of a recipe

AMOUNT PER SERVING	% DAILY VALUE
Calories: 278	14%
Calories from Fat: 180	27%
Total Fat: 21g	32%
Saturated Fat: 3g	15%
Cholesterol: 0mg	0%
Sodium: 594mg	25%
Total Carbohydrates: 14g	5%
Fiber: 0g	0%
Sugars: 0g	0%
Protein: 0g	0%
Vitamin A:	44%
Vitamin C:	256%
Calcium:	0%
Iron:	61%

Grilled Artichokes

INGREDIENTS

2 large artichokes, halved vertically
juice and zest from 1 large lemon
1 tablespoon olive oil
sea salt and pepper
1 cup chicken stock

DIRECTIONS

Place the artichoke halves in a bowl of water to cover and add the lemon juice. Pre heat the Flip Pan on medium high heat for 5 minutes per side.

Drain the artichokes and rub with olive oil and salt and pepper.

Place the artichokes cut side down on the grill side of the Flip Pan. Cook for 5 minutes.

Flip and cook for 3 minutes longer.

Add the chicken stock and lemon zest, close and cook for 20 minutes longer over medium high heat. Cut out the needle like center of the chokes, serve with a nice aoli or drawn butter.

Cook and Prep time 30 minutes

NUTRITION FACTS

Serving Size: ½ of a recipe

AMOUNT PER SERVING	% DAILY VALUE
Calories: 18	1%
Calories from Fat: 5	1%
Total Fat: 1g	2%
Saturated Fat: 0g	0%
Cholesterol: 0mg	0%
Sodium: 356mg	15%
Total Carbohydrates: 0g	0%
Fiber: 0g	0%
Sugars: 0g	0%
Protein: 2g	4%
Vitamin A:	0%
Vitamin C:	0%
Calcium:	0%
Iron:	0%

Herb Green Beans with Feta

INGREDIENTS

1½ pounds green beans, trimmed

1 teaspoon kosher salt

¼ cup olive oil

4 tablespoons torn fresh mint leaves, divided

2 tablespoons chopped fresh dill, divided

2 tablespoons lemon peel, in matchstick-size strips, divided

2 tablespoons fresh lemon juice

2 ounces feta, crumbled

freshly ground black pepper

DIRECTIONS

Place Flip Pan half filled with water over medium high heat.

When water comes to a boil about 3 minutes add the beans to the salted water just until crisp-tender, about 5 minutes with lid closed.

Drain green beans and transfer to a colander set in a bowl of ice water; let cool. Drain well, then pat dry with paper towels.

Toss beans, oil, 2 tablespoons mint, 1 tablespoon dill, 1 tablespoon lemon zest, 2 tablespoon lemon juice, and half of feta in a large bowl; season with salt, pepper, and more lemon juice, if desired.

Serve beans topped with remaining feta, 2 tablespoon mint, 1 tablespoon dill, and 1 tablespoon lemon zest.

NUTRITION FACTS

Serving Size: ⅛ of a recipe

AMOUNT PER SERVING	% DAILY VALUE
Calories: 74	4%
Calories from Fat: 60	9%
Total Fat: 7g	11%
Saturated Fat: 1g	5%
Cholesterol: 0mg	0%
Sodium: 556mg	23%
Total Carbohydrates: 3g	1%
Fiber: 1g	4%
Sugars: 1g	
Protein: 1g	2%
Vitamin A:	4%
Vitamin C:	3%
Calcium:	1%
Iron:	3%

Karen A Volin's Potatoes with Balsamic Vinegar and Olive Oil

Serves 2

INGREDIENTS

4 red bliss potatoes, sliced thin

1 teaspoon olive oil

¼ teaspoon sea salt

¼ teaspoon fresh, cracked pepper

1 teaspoon balsamic vinegar

DIRECTIONS

Preheat Flip Pan over medium heat top and bottom approximately 2 minutes per side.

Add the oil and heat for 1 minute.

Add the potatoes, salt pepper and vinegar.

Stir then close the Flip Pan and cook for 5 minutes per side or till golden brown.

NUTRITION FACTS

Serving Size: ½ of a recipe

AMOUNT PER SERVING	% DAILY VALUE
Calories: 195	10%
Calories from Fat: 20	3%
Total Fat: 3g	5%
Saturated Fat: 0g	0%
Cholesterol: 0mg	0%
Sodium: 309mg	13%
Total Carbohydrates: 40g	13%
Fiber: 4g	16%
Sugars: 2g	
Protein: 5g	9%
Vitamin A:	0%
Vitamin C:	29%
Calcium:	1%
Iron:	4%

Macaroni and Cheese with Bacon and Beer

Serves 4

INGREDIENTS

3 cups chicken stock

2 cups elbow macaroni

8 strips of bacon, cooked crispy then crumbled

⅓ cup Guinness

⅔ cup heavy cream

1½ cups Cheddar cheese

½ teaspoon black pepper

¼ teaspoon smoked paprika

pinch cayenne pepper

salt, to taste

½ cup toasted panko crumbs

¼ cup grated parmesan

DIRECTIONS

Place Flip Pan on medium high heat add in the chicken stock. Close the lid and bring to a boil.

Add the macaroni to the boiling chicken stock and close lid and cook for 7 minutes.

Add the beer, and cream, mix well and with the pasta.

Add the cheese, ¼ a cup at a time, Stir until cheese has melted before adding more.

Add the crumbled bacon and all spices, and stir.

Pour into gratin dish

Sprinkle with panko and parmesan and place under broiler to brown for 1–2 minutes.

NUTRITION FACTS

Serving Size: ¼ of a recipe

AMOUNT PER SERVING	% DAILY VALUE
Calories: 502	25%
Calories from Fat: 322	48%
Total Fat: 37g	57%
Saturated Fat: 19g	95%
Cholesterol: 109mg	36%
Sodium: 1020mg	43%
Total Carbohydrates: 20g	7%
Fiber: 3g	12%
Sugars: 0g	0%
Protein: 23g	42%
Vitamin A:	22%
Vitamin C:	0%
Calcium:	30%
Iron:	1%

Parmesan Crusted Eggplant

INGREDIENTS

2 medium eggplants cut in ½-inch rounds

½ tablespoon coarse sea salt

2 large eggs, beaten

2 cups Parmesan cheese, shredded

sea salt and freshly ground pepper

½ teaspoon Italian seasoning

nonstick spray

1 28-ounce can petite diced tomatoes

2 tablespoons extra virgin olive oil

4 medium cloves garlic, minced

¼ teaspoon red pepper flakes

½ cup fresh basil leaves, chopped

1 teaspoon salt

½ teaspoon pepper

8 ounces whole milk mozzarella or
    part-skim mozzarella, shredded (2 cups)

½ cup grated Parmesan cheese

10 fresh basil leaves, torn, for garnish

NUTRITION FACTS

Serving Size: ¼ of a recipe

AMOUNT PER SERVING	% DAILY VALUE
Calories: 389	19%
Calories from Fat: 298	45%
Total Fat: 31g	48%
Saturated Fat: 17g	85%
Cholesterol: 147mg	49%
Sodium: 2033mg	85%
Total Carbohydrates: 1g	0%
Fiber: 0g	0%
Sugars: 0g	0%
Protein: 34g	62%
Vitamin A:	3%
Vitamin C:	2%
Calcium:	91%
Iron:	1%

DIRECTIONS

Preheat oven to 350 degrees.

FOR THE EGGPLANT: Toss half of eggplant slices and 1½ teaspoons salt in large bowl until combined; transfer salted eggplant to large colander set over bowl. Repeat with remaining eggplant and salt, placing second batch in colander on top of first. Let stand until eggplant releases about 2 tablespoons liquid, 30 to 45 minutes. Arrange eggplant slices on triple layer paper towels; cover with another triple layer paper towels. Firmly press each

Continued >>

slice to remove as much liquid as possible, then wipe off excess salt.

Preheat Flip Pan, griddle side down, over medium heat. Dip each eggplant slice into the beaten egg, and then press into the Parmesan cheese. Spray the Flip Pan with nonstick spray then add the eggplant slices to the pan, sprinkle with salt and pepper and Italian seasonings, and cook for 3 minutes. Then flip and cook 3 minutes longer, remove to a plate, and repeat with remaining slices till all the eggplant has been encrusted with the Parmesan coating.

FOR THE SAUCE: Process half the diced tomatoes in food processor until almost smooth, about 5 seconds. Heat olive oil, garlic, and red pepper flakes in Dutch oven over medium-high heat, stirring occasionally, until fragrant and garlic is light golden, about 3 minutes; stir in processed and remaining can of diced tomatoes. Bring sauce to boil, then reduce heat to medium-low and simmer, stirring occasionally, until slightly thickened and reduced, about 15 minutes. Stir in basil and season to taste with salt and pepper.

TO ASSEMBLE: Spread 1 cup tomato sauce in bottom of Flip Pan. Layer in half of eggplant slices, overlapping slices to fit; distribute 1 cup sauce over eggplant; sprinkle with half of mozzarella. Layer in remaining eggplant and dot with 1 cup sauce, sprinkle with Parmesan and remaining mozzarella. Close the Flip Pan and place in center rack in the oven for 20 minutes, or flip on stove over medium for 10 minutes. Cool 10 minutes; scatter basil over top, and serve, passing remaining tomato sauce separately.

Pad Thai

INGREDIENTS

1 8-ounce box large rice noodle

3 cups hot, water

¼ cup peanuts

2 tablespoons fresh cilantro

1 red pepper, julienned

½ cup bean sprouts

For the sauce

3 tablespoons rice vinegar

1 tablespoons fresh lime juice

½ tablespoon brown sugar

2 tablespoons fish sauce

1 tablespoon soy sauce

¼ teaspoon cayenne pepper

⅛ teaspoon white pepper

NUTRITION FACTS

Serving Size: ½ of a recipe

AMOUNT PER SERVING	% DAILY VALUE
Calories: 110	6%
Calories from Fat: 73	11%
Total Fat: 9g	14%
Saturated Fat: 1g	5%
Cholesterol: 0mg	0%
Sodium: 55mg	2%
Total Carbohydrates: 5g	2%
Fiber: 0g	0%
Sugars: 1g	
Protein: 5g	9%
Vitamin A:	0%
Vitamin C:	26%
Calcium:	1%
Iron:	3%

DIRECTIONS

Soak the rice noodles in the hot water till tender.

Mix all the ingredients together for the sauce in a separate bowl.

Preheat Flip Pan top and bottom over medium heat.

Add all the ingredients, cook with lid closed 3 minutes per side.

Serve hot

Sun-Dried Tomato Pesto Tortellini

Serves 2

INGREDIENTS

1 cup chicken stock

1 pound fresh tortellini, filled with pesto or cheese

½ cup sun-dried tomato pesto (store bought or homemade)

¼ cup heavy cream

2 tablespoons freshly grated parmesan

5 artichoke hearts, quartered

3 basil leaves, torn

DIRECTIONS

Put the chicken stock in the Flip Pan, bring to a boil over medium high heat. About 3 minutes.

Add the tortellinis and close lid and cook for 4 minutes Pasta will puff up like pillows.

Remove from heat and stir in the remaining ingredients. Close lid and let rest 2 minutes.

Delicious!!!!

NUTRITION FACTS

Serving Size: ½ of a recipe

AMOUNT PER SERVING	% DAILY VALUE
Calories: 160	8%
Calories from Fat: 105	16%
Total Fat: 13g	20%
Saturated Fat: 6g	30%
Cholesterol: 40mg	13%
Sodium: 683mg	28%
Total Carbohydrates: 8g	3%
Fiber: 2g	8%
Sugars: 2g	
Protein: 5g	9%
Vitamin A:	11%
Vitamin C:	7%
Calcium:	3%
Iron:	7%

Original Flip Pan
Meats

Easy Street Tacos

Serves 4

INGREDIENTS

½ cup bottled or homemade salsa

2 teaspoons lemon juice

2 medium avocados, peeled, pitted and diced

1 medium tomato, chopped (about 1 cup)

2 green onions, sliced (about ¼ cup)

2 boneless chicken breasts

½ teaspoon salt

½ teaspoon chili powder

½ teaspoon cumin

nonstick spray

12 corn tortillas

¾ cup Cheddar cheese, shredded

sprig cilantro

¼ cup cabbage, shredded

1 jalapeno, sliced thin

NUTRITION FACTS

Serving Size: ¼ of a recipe

AMOUNT PER SERVING	% DAILY VALUE
Calories: 375	19%
Calories from Fat: 81	12%
Total Fat: 15g	23%
Saturated Fat: 5g	25%
Cholesterol: 36mg	12%
Sodium: 738mg	31%
Total Carbohydrates: 42g	14%
Fiber: 4g	16%
Sugars: 1g	
Protein: 11g	20%
Vitamin A:	31%
Vitamin C:	97%
Calcium:	21%
Iron:	28%

DIRECTIONS

Stir the salsa, lemon juice, avocado, tomato and onions in a medium bowl.

Place the Flip Pan on medium high burner and heat top and bottom, spray with nonstick

Cook the corn tortillas 3 minutes then flip cook 2 minutes longer, remove and cover to keep warm. Repeat with remaining tortillas till they are all cooked.

Season chicken, then place the breasts in the Flip Pan and cook for 5 minutes per side.

Remove to a cutting board, let rest a couple of minutes. Slice thin.

To assemble, place shredded cabbage in each tortilla, then top with sliced chicken

Top with the avocado mixture and the cheese. Roll the tortilla around the filling. Serve with additional salsa. Garnish with the cilantro leaves and fresh jalapenos

Cheese and Prosciutto Stuffed Chicken Breasts

serves 2

INGREDIENTS

2 boneless chicken breasts, butterflied

¼ cup spreadable garlic and herb cream cheese

4 thin slices prosciutto

2 tablespoons oil-packed sun-dried tomatoes, chopped

6–12 basil leaves, depending on size

2 tablespoons olive oil

salt and pepper, to taste

DIRECTIONS

Spread the chicken breasts open.

Spread ½ of the cream cheese on each chicken breast top with prosciutto and tomatoes and basil. Secure each breast with toothpicks. Season with salt and pepper.

Heat the olive oil in the Flip Pan over medium heat for 2 minutes add the chicken breasts and close the Flip Pan cook for 5 minutes, then flip and cook 5 minutes longer.

Remove to platter, be sure to take out the toothpicks before serving.

NUTRITION FACTS

Serving Size: ½ of a recipe

AMOUNT PER SERVING	% DAILY VALUE
Calories: 90	5%
Calories from Fat: 14	2%
Total Fat: 2g	3%
Saturated Fat: 0g	0%
Cholesterol: 27mg	9%
Sodium: 139mg	6%
Total Carbohydrates: 6g	2%
Fiber: 1g	4%
Sugars: 0g	0%
Protein: 11g	20%
Vitamin A:	20%
Vitamin C:	40%
Calcium:	0%
Iron:	4%

Moroccan Chicken

INGREDIENTS

2 tablespoons olive oil

1 whole chicken, cut into parts

½ teaspoon salt

½ teaspoon ground pepper

1 large onion, chopped

2 garlic cloves, minced

1 tablespoon lemon juice

4 preserved lemon slices

½ cup chicken stock

1 teaspoon paprika

¼ teaspoon ground turmeric

½ cup Kalamata olives

1 tablespoon fresh cilantro, chopped

DIRECTIONS

Place the Flip Pan on the stove and preheat over medium high.

Let heat for 2 minutes then add in the oil.

Pat the chicken with paper towels to remove the moisture. Season both sides with salt and pepper.

When the oil and pan are hot, carefully add the chicken and sear all sides. Cook for 5 minutes per side.

Add all the remaining ingredients except cilantro and stir.

Close lid and cook for 45 minutes.

Sprinkle with cilantro and serve.

I love to serve with couscous

Total Cook Time: 50 minutes

NUTRITION FACTS

Serving Size: ⅙ of a recipe

AMOUNT PER SERVING	% DAILY VALUE
Calories: 84	4%
Calories from Fat: 41	6%
Total Fat: 7g	11%
Saturated Fat: 1g	5%
Cholesterol: 0mg	0%
Sodium: 381mg	16%
Total Carbohydrates: 7g	2%
Fiber: 1g	4%
Sugars: 0g	0%
Protein: 1g	2%
Vitamin A:	7%
Vitamin C:	35%
Calcium:	2%
Iron:	0%

Grilled Chicken Cordon Blue

INGREDIENTS

4 skin-on, boneless chicken breasts,
   butterflied and lightly pounded
4 teaspoons Dijon mustard
1 sprig thyme, chopped
4 slices black forest ham
4 slices gruyere cheese
1 tablespoon olive oil
salt and pepper

DIRECTIONS

Cut into and across chicken but not all the way through. Pound out a bit then season inside with salt and pepper. Spread chicken with mustard and fill with ham and cheese, close chicken up, drizzle liberally with olive oil and season the skin and backside of breasts with salt and pepper. If the chicken seems overstuffed, secure with wet skewers or twine.

Preheat Flip Pan on medium high heat for 2 minutes per side.

Add the chicken breasts and cook for 5 minutes with Flip Pan closed.

Flip and cook 4 minutes longer.

NUTRITION FACTS

Serving Size: ¼ of a recipe

AMOUNT PER SERVING	% DAILY VALUE
Calories: 85	4%
Calories from Fat: 44	7%
Total Fat: 5g	8%
Saturated Fat: 1g	5%
Cholesterol: 27mg	9%
Sodium: 184mg	8%
Total Carbohydrates: 0g	0%
Fiber: 0g	0%
Sugars: 0g	0%
Protein: 10g	18%
Vitamin A:	0%
Vitamin C:	0%
Calcium:	0%
Iron:	2%

Maple Mustard Glazed Salmon

serves 6

INGREDIENTS

1½ pounds salmon fillet, cut into 6 equal pieces
¼ cup butter, melted
¼ cup maple syrup
2 tbsps. grainy, mustard
2 tablespoons soy sauce
pepper, to taste

DIRECTIONS

In a small bowl, whisk together the butter, maple syrup, mustard and soy sauce.

Preheat Flip Pan on medium heat, Place salmon flesh side down in Flip Pan, close and let cook for 3–4 minutes

Flip pan and open, spread sauce over the salmon, close the Flip Pan and cook 3 minutes longer.

NUTRITION FACTS

Serving Size: ⅙ of a recipe

AMOUNT PER SERVING	% DAILY VALUE
Calories: 980	49%
Calories from Fat: 458	69%
Total Fat: 51g	78%
Saturated Fat: 7g	35%
Cholesterol: 387mg	129%
Sodium: 351mg	15%
Total Carbohydrates: 9g	3%
Fiber: 0g	0%
Sugars: 6g	
Protein: 112g	204%
Vitamin A:	25%
Vitamin C:	0%
Calcium:	0%
Iron:	10%

92

Snapper Vera Cruz

INGREDIENTS

1 teaspoon olive oil

1 medium onion, chopped

½ green bell pepper, chopped

1 fresh jalapeño pepper, chopped,
   with half the seeds removed (for less heat)

1 tablespoon tomato paste

1 14¾-ounce can diced tomatoes, drained

½ cup dry white wine

1 tablespoon fresh lime juice

3 tablespoons capers, drained

1 tablespoon fresh cilantro, chopped

2 garlic cloves, minced

¼ teaspoon salt, plus more to taste

2 pounds fresh red snapper fillets

freshly ground black pepper

DIRECTIONS

Pre heat Flip Pan top and bottom over medium high add the oil

Add the onions and peppers and close Flip Pan and cook for 3 minutes.

Add the paste and tomatoes and jalapenos, close Flip Pan and cook for 2 minutes longer.

Stir then add the remaining ingredients and close Flip Pan and cook for 6 minutes longer.

NUTRITION FACTS

Serving Size: ¼ of a recipe

AMOUNT PER SERVING	% DAILY VALUE
Calories: 61	3%
Calories from Fat: 10	1%
Total Fat: 1g	2%
Saturated Fat: 0g	0%
Cholesterol: 0mg	0%
Sodium: 620mg	26%
Total Carbohydrates: 10g	3%
Fiber: 1g	4%
Sugars: 1g	
Protein: 1g	2%
Vitamin A:	15%
Vitamin C:	34%
Calcium:	0%
Iron:	2%

Mongolian Beef Stir Fry

serves 6

Delicious dinner in a snap

INGREDIENTS

2 pounds flank steak

½ cup cornstarch

½ cup vegetable oil

2 tablespoons vegetable oil

1 cup soy sauce

1 cup brown sugar

4 cloves garlic, minced

1 cup water

2 or 3 green onions, chopped

DIRECTIONS

Slice the steak into small thin pieces against the grain. In a large plastic bag add the starch and add the beef to it. Close the plastic bag and shake really well until each pieces is coated with cornstarch. Refrigerate until ready to use.

In a small sauce pan add the oil, soy sauce, brown sugar, garlic and water. Stir and cook over medium heat until sauce thickens. It took me about 20 minutes until the sauce thickened and reduced. Set aside.

Place the Flip Pan on a medium high burner add oil. When the oil is hot, add half the meat let cook for two minutes with lid open, turn the meat to brown all sides, remove to a platter and add the remaining beef and repeat.

Add the cooked beef and add the sauce. Close the lid on the Flip Pan, shaking occasionally lower heat to medium and cook for 5 minutes.

Serve over rice and garnish with green onions.

NUTRITION FACTS

Serving Size: ⅙ of a recipe

AMOUNT PER SERVING	% DAILY VALUE
Calories: 399	115%
Calories from Fat: 960	144%
Total Fat: 113g	173%
Saturated Fat: 16g	80%
Cholesterol: 0mg	0%
Sodium: 8665mg	361%
Total Carbohydrates: 318g	106%
Fiber: 4g	15%
Sugars: 224g	
Protein: 42g	77%
Vitamin A:	0%
Vitamin C:	40%
Calcium:	0%
Iron:	0%

Braised Baby Back Ribs

Serves 2

INGREDIENTS

½ slab baby back ribs
1 tablespoon olive oil
½ teaspoon sea salt
½ teaspoon freshly ground pepper
¼ teaspoon smoked paprika
¼ teaspoon garlic salt
½ teaspoon brown sugar
1 cup hard cider ale or apple cider
1 cup barbecue sauce

DIRECTIONS

Rub the ribs with oil.

Combine all the seasoning and rub the meaty side of the ribs well.

Preheat oven to 350 degrees.

Preheat Flip Pan for 2–3 minutes per side on medium high heat.

Place the ribs meat side down on grill side of the Flip Pan.

Close Flip Pan and cook for 5 minutes.

Flip the pan and cook for 5 minutes longer.

Place Flip Pan in the oven and cook ribs for 1 hours.

Ribs should be falling off the bone. Cover with sauce.

Cook & prep time 90 minutes

NUTRITION FACTS

Serving Size: ½ of a recipe

AMOUNT PER SERVING	% DAILY VALUE
Calories: 64	3%
Calories from Fat: 0	0%
Total Fat: 0g	0%
Saturated Fat: 0g	0%
Cholesterol: 0mg	0%
Sodium: 883mg	37%
Total Carbohydrates: 16g	5%
Fiber: 0g	0%
Sugars: 14g	
Protein: 0g	0%
Vitamin A:	5%
Vitamin C:	0%
Calcium:	0%
Iron:	1%

95

Braised Apple-Cider Stuffed Pork Chops

Serves 6

INGREDIENTS

2 tablespoons olive oil

4 center cut pork chops, 2-inches thick, butterflied

1 teaspoon salt

½ teaspoon ground pepper

¼ cup salted butter

1 large apple, cored and diced

1 6-ounce package corn bread stuffing

4 fresh sage leaves, chopped

2 cups apple cider

1 teaspoon apple cider vinegar

2 tablespoons chicken stock

DIRECTIONS

Place the Flip Pan on burner set for medium high.

Let heat for 2 minutes then add in the oil.

Pat the pork chops with paper towels to remove the moisture. Season both sides with salt.

When the oil and pan are hot, carefully add the pork chops and sear all sides.

Transfer pork chops to a platter.

Add butter to the Flip Pan and heat the diced apples.

Add corn bread stuffing, sage and 1 cup of cider. Stir well.

Divide mixture and stuff each chop then place back into the Flip Pan.

Add the remaining ingredients and close the lid.

Cook over medium to medium high for 25 minutes.

When cook time is complete, carefully remove the chops to a platter.

Place the Flip Pan on a medium high burner and reduce the cooking liquid by half. Pour sauce over chops and serve hot.

NUTRITION FACTS

Serving Size: ⅙ of a recipe

AMOUNT PER SERVING	% DAILY VALUE
Calories: 320	16%
Calories from Fat: 170	26%
Total Fat: 18g	28%
Saturated Fat: 5g	25%
Cholesterol: 69mg	23%
Sodium: 548mg	23%
Total Carbohydrates: 16g	5%
Fiber: 1g	4%
Sugars: 10g	
Protein: 0g	0%
Vitamin A:	5%
Vitamin C:	1%
Calcium:	0%
Iron:	7%

Bacon Cheddar Burger

Delicious burger with bacon and cheese in every bite.

INGREDIENTS

1 pound ground beef chuck
½ pound bacon, chopped and cooked crisp
1 tablespoon onion, minced
¼ cup Cheddar cheese, shredded
pinch salt
pinch pepper

DIRECTIONS

Preheat the Flip Pan over medium heat. And the diced bacon and cook till crunchy golden brown about 3 minutes. Remove from pan and drain on a paper towel.

Add the onions to the Flip Pan and cook for 1 minute with Flip Pan closed, add them to paper towel to drain.

I a large bowl, add the remaining ingredients and the bacon and onions and gently mix with your hands.

Divide the ingredients into 4 equal patties.

Cook the patties in the Flip Pan for 4 minutes flip then cook for 4 minutes longer for medium.

Serve on a bun with lettuce tomato and avocado slices.

NUTRITION FACTS

Serving Size: ¼ of a recipe

AMOUNT PER SERVING	% DAILY VALUE
Calories: 115	6%
Calories from Fat: 95	14%
Total Fat: 10g	15%
Saturated Fat: 4g	20%
Cholesterol: 20mg	7%
Sodium: 295mg	12%
Total Carbohydrates: 0g	0%
Fiber: 0g	0%
Sugars: 0g	0%
Protein: 7g	13%
Vitamin A:	2%
Vitamin C:	0%
Calcium:	5%
Iron:	0%

Spatchcock Chicken

Serves 2

INGREDIENTS

2 tablespoons olive oil

1 whole chicken, backbone cut out and split

½ teaspoon salt

½ teaspoon ground pepper

1 large onion, chopped

2 garlic cloves, minced

1 tablespoon lemon juice

½ cup chicken stock

1 sprig thyme

DIRECTIONS

Preheat oven to 350 degrees

Place the Flip Pan on the stove and preheat over medium for 3 minutes per side.

With grill side facing up add in the oil.

Pat the chicken with paper towels to remove the moisture. Season both sides with salt and pepper.

When the oil and pan are hot, carefully add the chicken. Close the lid, cook for 5 minutes; flip and cook 5 minutes longer.

Add all the remaining ingredients and stir.

Close the lid and cook 20 minutes longer without flipping

Total Cook Time: 20 minutes

NUTRITION FACTS

Serving Size: ½ of a recipe

AMOUNT PER SERVING	% DAILY VALUE
Calories: 243	12%
Calories from Fat: 120	18%
Total Fat: 20g	31%
Saturated Fat: 2g	10%
Cholesterol: 0mg	0%
Sodium: 963mg	40%
Total Carbohydrates: 20g	7%
Fiber: 2g	8%
Sugars: 0g	0%
Protein: 1g	2%
Vitamin A:	20%
Vitamin C:	105%
Calcium:	5%
Iron:	0%

Crab Cakes

INGREDIENTS

2 tablespoons unsalted butter

2 tablespoons olive oil

¾ cup red onion, diced (1 small onion)

1½ cups diced celery (4 stalks)

½ cup diced red bell pepper (1 small pepper)

½ cup diced yellow bell pepper (1 small pepper)

¼ cup fresh flat-leaf parsley, minced

1 tablespoon capers, drained

¼ teaspoon hot pepper sauce (recommended: Tabasco)

½ teaspoon Worcestershire sauce

1½ teaspoons crab boil seasonings (recommended: Old Bay)

½ teaspoon kosher salt

½ teaspoon freshly ground black pepper

½ pound lump crabmeat, drained and picked to remove shells

½ cup plain dry bread crumbs

½ cup good mayonnaise

2 teaspoons Dijon mustard

2 extra-large eggs, lightly beaten

½ cup panko

NUTRITION FACTS

Serving Size: ⅙ of a recipe

AMOUNT PER SERVING	% DAILY VALUE
Calories: 289	14%
Calories from Fat: 224	34%
Total Fat: 25g	38%
Saturated Fat: 3g	15%
Cholesterol: 88mg	29%
Sodium: 742mg	31%
Total Carbohydrates: 10g	3%
Fiber: 1g	4%
Sugars: 0g	0%
Protein: 7g	13%
Vitamin A:	4%
Vitamin C:	12%
Calcium:	6%
Iron:	6%

DIRECTIONS

Preheat Flip Pan top and bottom over medium heat.

Add the butter oil and heat 2 minutes longer.

Add the onions and peppers and cook till tender. About 2 minutes with pan closed.

Place in a large bowl and allow to cool.

Add all the remaining except panko cooked vegetables and gently mix by hand.

Cover and chill in the refrigerator for 30 minutes.

Form batter into ½ cup patties and coat with panko

Pre heat the Flip Pan top and bottom over medium high heat, spray well with nonstick spray.

Add crab cakes and cook for 4 minutes flip and cook for 3 minutes longer or till golden brown.

Prep Time: 30 min

Josephine Cook's Chicken Francaise

Serves 2

INGREDIENTS

1 pound boneless, skinless chicken breast
2 eggs
1 tablespoon milk
½ cup flour seasoned with salt and pepper
3 tablespoons extra virgin olive oil
½ stick butter
2 medium lemons
2 teaspoons lemon zest
½ cup white wine
½ cup chicken stock or broth
½ cup fresh parsley, chopped
salt and pepper

DIRECTIONS

Slice the chicken breast into thin chicken cutlets or use flattened chicken tenders

Mix flour with salt and pepper

Beat eggs, milk and some salt and pepper

NUTRITION FACTS

Serving Size: ½ of a recipe

AMOUNT PER SERVING	% DAILY VALUE
Calories: 402	20%
Calories from Fat: 253	38%
Total Fat: 28g	43%
Saturated Fat: 2g	10%
Cholesterol: 250mg	83%
Sodium: 1006mg	42%
Total Carbohydrates: 14g	5%
Fiber: 1g	4%
Sugars: 0g	0%
Protein: 22g	40%
Vitamin A:	20%
Vitamin C:	47%
Calcium:	4%
Iron:	7%

Dip the chicken in seasoned flour, set aside

Preheat Flip Pan on both sides for 3 minutes over medium heat

Open the lid and add 3 TB of the Extra Virgin Olive Oil (I put it in the grill side of the pan)

When the oil is hot, dip the seasoned chicken cutlets into the egg mixture, on both sides

With the lid open, cook the chicken until a golden color, remove and keep warm.

Add ½ stick of butter in the pan.

Add lemon juice, lemon zest, stock or broth, and wine.

Close lid and cook 5 minutes, on medium heat, to reduce the sauce.

Open the lid check for seasonings, if more salt or pepper is needed add some now. Add the chicken, turning to cover with all of the sauce.

Add the parsley.

Close the lid and reduce the heat to medium low, cook 10 more min

Ginger Beef with Brussels Sprouts

INGREDIENTS

1 pound top sirloin, cut into thin strips
1 tablespoon sesame oil
1 small onion, sliced
3 cloves garlic, sliced
1 inch of ginger, peeled and minced
2 tablespoons soy sauce
1 tablespoon rice vinegar
1 tablespoon honey
1 teaspoon crushed red pepper flakes (optional)
1 red pepper, julienned
12 brussel sprouts, halved
¼ cup orange juice
½ tablespoon cornstarch

DIRECTIONS

Preheat Flip Pan top and bottom over medium heat.

Place the sirloin, oil, onion, garlic, ginger, soy sauce, and vinegar in the Flip Pan. Stir and close the lid.

Set timer for 15 minutes.

When the cook cycle is complete, add the honey, peppers, and Brussels sprouts.

Close the lid and cook 5 minutes longer.

Dissolve the cornstarch in the orange juice.

When cook time is complete open the lid and stir in the cornstarch mixture, stir till thickened.

Serve over rice.

Cook Time 18 minutes

NUTRITION FACTS

Serving Size: ¼ of a recipe

AMOUNT PER SERVING	% DAILY VALUE
Calories: 73	4%
Calories from Fat: 30	4%
Total Fat: 4g	6%
Saturated Fat: 1g	5%
Cholesterol: 0mg	0%
Sodium: 273mg	11%
Total Carbohydrates: 10g	3%
Fiber: 1g	4%
Sugars: 6g	
Protein: 3g	5%
Vitamin A:	0%
Vitamin C:	13%
Calcium:	0%
Iron:	0%

Korean Style Beef Short Ribs

INGREDIENTS

1 tablespoon olive oil

3 pounds beef short ribs

½ teaspoon salt

1 medium onion, chopped

4 gloves garlic, minced

1 teaspoon ginger, grated

1 cup beef stock

¼ cup brown sugar

2 tablespoon rice wine vinegar

¼ cup soy sauce

1 Asian pear peeled and diced

2 green onions, sliced thin (garnish)

DIRECTIONS

Preheat oven to 350 degrees.

Place the Flip Pan onto stove and set to medium-high heat.

Let heat for 2 minutes, then add in the oil and heat 2 minutes longer.

Pat the ribs with paper towels to remove the moisture. Season both sides with salt.

When the oil and pot are hot, carefully add the ribs and sear all sides with no lid.

Add all the remaining ingredients and stir.

Close Flip Pan lid and place in the oven. Set timer for 3 hours.

At the end of 3 hours ribs will be tender. Carefully remove the ribs to a platter.

Place the Flip Pan back on the stove. Skim fat from sauce and reduce the cooking liquid by half, approximately 5 minutes.

NUTRITION FACTS

Serving Size: ⅙ of a recipe.

AMOUNT PER SERVING	% DAILY VALUE
Calories: 564	28%
Calories from Fat: 198	30%
Total Fat: 25g	38%
Saturated Fat: 7g	35%
Cholesterol: 196mg	65%
Sodium: 1730mg	72%
Total Carbohydrates: 13g	4%
Fiber: 2g	8%
Sugars: 4g	
Protein: 74g	135%
Vitamin A:	294%
Vitamin C:	15%
Calcium:	2%
Iron:	36%

Buffalo Chicken Burgers

INGREDIENTS

1½ pounds ground chicken

¼ cup carrot, grated

¼ cup celery, finely diced

2 tablespoons red onions, finely diced

¼ cup blue cheese, crumbled (optional)

¼ cup buffalo hot sauce, or to taste

salt and pepper, to taste

3 tablespoons blue cheese or ranch dressing

4 buns

4 leaves Bibb lettuce

4 slices tomato

DIRECTIONS

Mix the chicken, carrot, celery, onion, blue cheese, hot sauce, salt and pepper and form into 4 patties.

Preheat the Flip Pan over medium heat and heat top and bottom for 3 minutes per side.

Place the patties into the flip and cook for 4 minutes per side.

Cover with additional hot sauce and cheese crumbles if desired and close Flip Pan and cook 1 minute longer.

Serve the buffalo chicken burgers in the buns along with lettuce, tomatoes, and blue cheese dressing.

Prep Time: 10 minutes

NUTRITION FACTS

Serving Size: ¼ of a recipe

AMOUNT PER SERVING	% DAILY VALUE
Calories: 143	7%
Calories from Fat: 34	5%
Total Fat: 4g	6%
Saturated Fat: 1g	5%
Cholesterol: 43mg	14%
Sodium: 569mg	24%
Total Carbohydrates: 2g	1%
Fiber: 1g	4%
Sugars: 0g	0%
Protein: 24g	44%
Vitamin A:	25%
Vitamin C:	12%
Calcium:	4%
Iron:	0%

Georgina Budney's Crab Stuffed Flounder

Serves 4

INGREDIENTS

2 pounds flounder

1 stick of butter

4 slices fresh white bread

1 small onion, diced

1 celery stalk, diced

8 ounces of crab meat

DIRECTIONS

Stuffing: Use a food processor and place the bread in and pulse to make coarse crumbs. Dice the onion and celery.

Heat the Flip Pan on both sides for a few minutes on low/medium heat. Open the lid and place the diced onions and celery in and sauté for 3 minutes. Put quarter of butter in and stir. When the butter is melted place bread crumbs in. Let it absorb butter, then add in the crab meat. Close lid for 5 minutes. Flip pan and cook another 5 minutes. Done.

Rinse flounder. Pat dry. Place a spoonful of stuffing mixture in flounder and roll. Place all in bottom of Flip Pan. Melt rest of butter and spread on top of flounder. Sprinkle some paprika on top. Cut lemon and place on top. Close lid.

Cook on low heat on the stove top. 15 minutes later flounder should be white in appearance. Done.

NUTRITION FACTS

Serving Size: ¼ of a recipe

AMOUNT PER SERVING	% DAILY VALUE
Calories: 231	12%
Calories from Fat: 205	31%
Total Fat: 23g	35%
Saturated Fat: 0g	0%
Cholesterol: 95mg	32%
Sodium: 385mg	16%
Total Carbohydrates: 1g	0%
Fiber: 0g	0%
Sugars: 0g	0%
Protein: 6g	11%
Vitamin A:	16%
Vitamin C:	5%
Calcium:	1%
Iron:	3%

Jill Allmandinger Moyer's Breaded Pork Chops

Serves 4

INGREDIENTS

4 pork chops
3 eggs, beaten lightly
3 tablespoons milk
1½ cups Italian bread crumbs
½ cup shredded Parmesan cheese
salt and pepper
2 tablespoons garlic herb oil (or olive oil)
¼ cup chicken stock

DIRECTIONS

Beat the egg with the milk, set aside.

Mix the bread crumbs, salt and pepper with the Parmesan cheese.

Preheat the Flip Pan on both sides, medium heat for a few minutes.

Dredge the pork chops in the egg and milk mixture.

Dip them in the Italian bread crumb and cheese mixture.

Open the lid and add the garlic herb oil

Add the chops, close the lid, Cook for 5 minutes, on medium high heat.

Open the lid and manually flip the chops.

Add some stock to assist with cooking.

Close the lid and cook 5 more minutes

Open the lid and check to see if pork chops are cooked.

NUTRITION FACTS

Serving Size: ¼ of a recipe

AMOUNT PER SERVING	% DAILY VALUE
Calories: 309	15%
Calories from Fat: 159	24%
Total Fat: 15g	23%
Saturated Fat: 10g	50%
Cholesterol: 195mg	65%
Sodium: 312mg	13%
Total Carbohydrates: 0g	0%
Fiber: 0g	0%
Sugars: 0g	0%
Protein: 9g	16%
Vitamin A:	3%
Vitamin C:	0%
Calcium:	19%
Iron:	11%

Curry in a Hurry

INGREDIENTS

1½ tablespoons olive oil

1 small yellow onion, thinly sliced

2 cloves garlic, minced

1-inch piece ginger, minced

½ teaspoon turmeric

½ teaspoon cumin

½ teaspoon cayenne pepper

2 teaspoons curry powder

½ cup plain Greek yogurt

¾ cup heavy cream

½ teaspoon kosher salt

¼ teaspoon black pepper

1 14.5-ounce can diced tomatoes, drained

meat from 1 rotisserie chicken, sliced or shredded

¼ cup fresh cilantro leaves, roughly chopped

NUTRITION FACTS

Serving Size: ⅙ of a recipe

AMOUNT PER SERVING	% DAILY VALUE
Calories: 142	7%
Calories from Fat: 130	19%
Total Fat: 16g	25%
Saturated Fat: 7g	35%
Cholesterol: 40mg	13%
Sodium: 255mg	11%
Total Carbohydrates: 2g	1%
Fiber: 0g	0%
Sugars: 1g	
Protein: 2g	4%
Vitamin A:	9%
Vitamin C:	2%
Calcium:	3%
Iron:	0%

DIRECTIONS

Place the Flip Pan on stove over medium high heat.

Heat the oil in pan for 1 minute. Add the onion and cook closed for 4 minutes.

Sprinkle with the, turmeric, cumin, and cayenne and curry powder and close lid and cook, for 1 minute.

Add the yogurt and cream and simmer gently for 3 minutes. Stir in the salt, pepper, and tomatoes and chicken. Close the lid and cook for 2 minutes.

Remove from heat.

Serve over rice and sprinkle with the cilantro

Cook Time: 20 minutes

Original Flip Pan
Breakfast

Sausage n Biscuits

INGREDIENTS

12 ounces of buttermilk biscuit dough

6 eggs

2 cups peppered gravy

1 pound sausage, cooked and drained

1 cup cheese, shredded

½ cup milk

salt and pepper, to taste

DIRECTIONS

Preheat oven to 350.

Preheat Flip Pan over medium heat top and bottom.

Spray Flip Pan well with nonstick spray top and bottom.

Cut biscuit dough into 1-inch pieces, and line the bottom of the pan.

Layer cooked sausage over the biscuit pieces.

Layer shredded cheese over sausage.

Whisk eggs and milk, add salt and pepper and pour over biscuit/layers.

Pour gravy over everything.

Bake for 30–45 minutes, or until eggs and biscuits are cooked through.

Serve warm

Cook Time: 50 minutes

NUTRITION FACTS

Serving Size: ¼ of a recipe

AMOUNT PER SERVING	% DAILY VALUE
Calories: 806	40%
Calories from Fat: 472	71%
Total Fat: 52g	80%
Saturated Fat: 18g	90%
Cholesterol: 338mg	113%
Sodium: 2499mg	104%
Total Carbohydrates: 47g	16%
Fiber: 3g	12%
Sugars: 5g	
Protein: 30g	55%
Vitamin A:	7%
Vitamin C:	1%
Calcium:	6%
Iron:	29%

Abuela's Tortilla de Patatass by Nicolas Torre

Servings: 4

INGREDIENTS

4 large potatoes, peeled and diced
1 sweet onion, diced
1 teaspoon salt
6 large eggs
1 tablespoon olive oil

DIRECTIONS

Toss the potatoes and onions in olive oil.

Preheat the Flip Pan top and bottom over medium high heat.

Add the potatoes and onions close Flip Pan and cook for 5 minutes per side.

Whisk eggs and salt until frothy

When potatoes and onions are golden brown remove them from Flip Pan and mix
With eggs.

Return them immediately to warm Flip Pan (on medium-high heat)

Close pan and cook for 2 minutes flip over and cook for another 2 minutes

Open to check—should be light golden on both sides.

When golden brown, cut in quarters and remove from Flip Pan

Top with choice of tomato sauce if desired.

NUTRITION FACTS

Serving Size: ¼ of a recipe

AMOUNT PER SERVING	% DAILY VALUE
Calories: 188	9%
Calories from Fat: 70	11%
Total Fat: 8g	12%
Saturated Fat: 2g	10%
Cholesterol: 215mg	72%
Sodium: 72mg	3%
Total Carbohydrates: 20g	7%
Fiber: 2g	8%
Sugars: 1g	
Protein: 8g	15%
Vitamin A:	6%
Vitamin C:	15%
Calcium:	3%
Iron:	6%

Ann Marie Shuta's Old Fashioned Rice Pudding

Serves 4

INGREDIENTS

4 cups cooked white rice
3 cups milk
1½ tablespoons butter
¼ teaspoon salt
3 eggs plus 1 yolk, beaten
½ cup sugar
1½ teaspoons vanilla
1 teaspoon lemon rind zest
½ teaspoon orange rind zest
½ cup dried cranberries

DIRECTIONS

Preheat oven to 350 degrees.

Combine all ingredients into bottom of Flip Pan. Bring to a boil on top of stove. Cover with shallow side of Flip Pan, then place pan in oven that has been preheated to 350 degrees. Bake for
1 hour or until pudding sets and does not look wet in the middle. Allow pudding to cool before slicing. It will cut like a cake.

NUTRITION FACTS

Serving Size: ¼ of a recipe

AMOUNT PER SERVING	% DAILY VALUE
Calories: 886	44%
Calories from Fat: 106	16%
Total Fat: 12g	18%
Saturated Fat: 3g	15%
Cholesterol: 134mg	45%
Sodium: 353mg	15%
Total Carbohydrates: 176g	59%
Fiber: 4g	16%
Sugars: 45g	
Protein: 9g	16%
Vitamin A:	14%
Vitamin C:	3%
Calcium:	30%
Iron:	26%

Asparagus Omelet

Serves 2

INGREDIENTS

10 ounces asparagus, cut into ⅓-inch pieces and steamed
6 large eggs
⅓ cup finely grated parmesan cheese
½ teaspoon salt
¼ teaspoon ground black pepper
1 tablespoon butter
1 tablespoon green onions, white parts only, thinly sliced

DIRECTIONS

Whisk eggs, grated Parmesan cheese, ½ teaspoon salt and ¼ teaspoon pepper in large bowl to blend well.

Preheat the Flip Pan over medium high heat top and bottom about 2 minutes per side.

Spray the Flip Pan well with nonstick spray.

Add the butter and allow to melt about 2 minutes longer.

Add asparagus, close the Flip Pan and cook for 3 minutes or till tender.

Spread asparagus mixture in single layer in Flip Pan with griddle side facing up.

Pour egg mixture over asparagus. Close Flip Pan and shaking pan occasionally until eggs are very softly set about 3 minutes.

Flip the Flip Pan and cook 3 minutes longer.

Roll omelet out onto platter.

Cook time 10 minutes

NUTRITION FACTS

Serving Size: ½ of a recipe

AMOUNT PER SERVING	% DAILY VALUE
Calories: 218	11%
Calories from Fat: 130	19%
Total Fat: 15g	23%
Saturated Fat: 3g	15%
Cholesterol: 445mg	148%
Sodium: 765mg	32%
Total Carbohydrates: 5g	2%
Fiber: 0g	0%
Sugars: 0g	0%
Protein: 12g	22%
Vitamin A:	28%
Vitamin C:	80%
Calcium:	4%
Iron:	28%

117

Strawberry Cream Cheese Stuffed French Toast

Serves 2

Tender warm french toast with the sweet and creamy filling is delious anytime . . .

INGREDIENTS

2 large eggs, beaten

⅓ cup whole, milk

¼ teaspoon ground nutmeg

¼ teaspoon salt

3 teaspoons sugar

¼ cup fresh strawberries, sliced

4 tablespoons berry flavored whipped cream cheese

4 2-inch slices of challah, preferably a few days old

DIRECTIONS

In a shallow bowl mix the eggs, milk, nutmeg salt and sugar.

Combine the fresh berries and whipped cream cheese in a small bowl.

Cut a slit into the top crust of each slice of bread and using a spoon stuff each piece of bread with 2 tablespoons of berry mixture.

Soak each piece of bread in the egg mixture till the entire slice is covered with the custard.

Preheat Flip Pan on griddle side over medium for 2–3 minutes, then spray with non-stick spray, flip and preheat grill side for 3 minutes longer.

Flip again and place each piece of bread on the griddle surface.

Cook for 3–4 minutes, then flip again and cook 3 minutes longer.

Serve hot with Maple syrup and butter dust with powdered sugar and more berries.

Cook Time: 20 minutes

NUTRITION FACTS

Serving Size: ½ of a recipe

AMOUNT PER SERVING	% DAILY VALUE
Calories: 97	5%
Calories from Fat: 34	5%
Total Fat: 4g	6%
Saturated Fat: 2g	10%
Cholesterol: 147mg	49%
Sodium: 359mg	15%
Total Carbohydrates: 10g	3%
Fiber: 0g	0%
Sugars: 8g	
Protein: 5g	9%
Vitamin A:	6%
Vitamin C:	17%
Calcium:	7%
Iron:	3%

Peanut Butter & Banana Stuffed French Toast

Serves 1

INGREDIENTS

1 banana, sliced

2 slices cinnamon swirl bread, sliced thick

2 tablespoons smooth peanut butter

2 eggs

⅛ cup of heavy cream

½ tablespoon vanilla

½ tablespoon cinnamon

¼ teaspoon nutmeg

dash of salt

1 tablespoon butter

nonstick spray

NUTRITION FACTS

Serving Size: 1 of a recipe

AMOUNT PER SERVING	% DAILY VALUE
Calories: 460	23%
Calories from Fat: 173	26%
Total Fat: 21g	32%
Saturated Fat: 8g	40%
Cholesterol: 327mg	109%
Sodium: 1202mg	50%
Total Carbohydrates: 56g	19%
Fiber: 5g	19%
Sugars: 4g	
Protein: 13g	23%
Vitamin A:	16%
Vitamin C:	13%
Calcium:	7%
Iron:	19%

DIRECTIONS

In a bowl (one that will be easy to fit the sandwich), combine your eggs, heavy cream, vanilla, cinnamon, nutmeg and a dash of salt. Gently whip until the eggs have been scrambled and everything is combined.

Now for the sandwich! Spread a thin layer of peanut butter on each slice of bread, place your sliced banana on one slice, and put the sandwich together!

Pre heat Flip Pan on medium heat top and bottom about 2 minutes per side.

Add tablespoon of butter and spray both sides with nonstick spray.

Dip your sandwich in the egg mixture, coating each side and then Place in the Flip Pan and cook 3 minutes flip and cook 3 minutes longer.

Serve with a dabble of whip cream while dusted with powder sugar and syrup for sure.

Corned Beef Hash

INGREDIENTS

2 cups diced cooked potatoes

1 pound cooked corned beef, diced

1 cup onion, diced

1 red bell pepper, diced

2 tablespoons olive oil

1 teaspoon salt

½ teaspoon celery salt

½ teaspoon garlic powder

½ teaspoon black pepper

DIRECTIONS

Preheat Flip Pan top and bottom over medium heat.

Add the oil, let heat 2 minutes longer.

Add the onion and bell pepper to the Flip Pan. Close and shake occasionally for 2 minutes.

Add potatoes and close the lid and let cook 3 minutes then flip and cook three minutes longer.

Stir in corned beef and salt and pepper and seasonings, Close the Flip Pan then cook3 minutes longer per side.

If desired, make 4 holes in hash and break 1 egg into each. Close the Flip Pan and over moderately low heat, cook, 5 minutes, or until eggs are cooked to desired doneness, and season with salt and pepper.

Cook time 15 minutes

NUTRITION FACTS

Serving Size: ¼ of a recipe

AMOUNT PER SERVING	% DAILY VALUE
Calories: 366	18%
Calories from Fat: 180	27%
Total Fat: 21g	32%
Saturated Fat: 1g	5%
Cholesterol: 100mg	33%
Sodium: 1753mg	73%
Total Carbohydrates: 10g	3%
Fiber: 1g	4%
Sugars: 0g	0%
Protein: 31g	56%
Vitamin A:	0%
Vitamin C:	7%
Calcium:	0%
Iron:	18%

Kelly Shaide Keene's Breakfast Pizza

You can go all veggie with this, all real pizza, what ever you have the feeling for. The crust is delightfully flaky and crisp. Note—do try to keep moisture to a minimum.

INGREDIENTS

6 eggs

1 tablespoon chopped onion

1 tablespoon mushrooms, chopped

1 tablespoon mini sweet peppers, thinly sliced

¼ cup precooked any combo or all of ham, sausage, turkey or chicken, chopped

1 tablespoon thinly sliced and quartered tomato

1 canister of crescent rolls

1 to 2 cups of any one or all of cheddar, mozzarella, or Monterey jack cheese, grated

8 sliced precooked crisp bacon, crumbled

salt and pepper, to taste

NUTRITION FACTS

Serving Size: ¼ of a recipe

AMOUNT PER SERVING	% DAILY VALUE
Calories: 123	6%
Calories from Fat: 46	7%
Total Fat: 5g	8%
Saturated Fat: 2g	10%
Cholesterol: 232mg	77%
Sodium: 98mg	4%
Total Carbohydrates: 4g	1%
Fiber: 1g	4%
Sugars: 0g	0%
Protein: 16g	29%
Vitamin A:	11%
Vitamin C:	16%
Calcium:	2%
Iron:	6%

DIRECTIONS

Preheat oven 350 degrees

Prepare onion, mushrooms, peppers, choice of meat and place in bowl.

Scramble eggs to cooked but still slightly custard like not completely done, but not runny.

Set aside eggs on plate.

Rolls out the crescent roll dough not tearing it in the precuts. Lay in deep side of Flip Pan

Make to fit entire bottom and up sides of Flip Pan.

Add scrambled eggs over crescent roll dough in pan, then cover with onion, mushrooms, peppers, and choice of meat.

Add sliced and quartered tomato and then cover with cheese.

Top with crumbled bacon.

Bake with lid closed in preheated oven 350 degrees for 30 minutes.

You can go all veggie with this, all real pizza, whatever you have the feeling for. The crust is delightfully flaky and crisp.

NOTE: try to keep moisture to a minimum

Blueberry Cream Cheese Stuffed French Toast with Corn Flake Crust

Serves 4

Thick stuffed French Toast filled with Cream Cheese and berries

INGREDIENTS

large egg, beaten

⅓ cup whole milk

¼ teaspoon ground nutmeg

¼ teaspoon salt

3 teaspoons sugar

¼ cup fresh blueberries

4 tablespoons berry flavored whipped cream cheese

4 2-inch slices of challah bread, preferably a few days old

1½ cups cornflakes, crumbled

DIRECTIONS

In a shallow bowl mix the eggs, milk, nutmeg salt and sugar.

Combine the fresh berries and whipped cream cheese in a small bowl.

Cut a slit into the top crust of each slice of bread and using a spoon stuff each piece of bread with 2 tablespoons of berry mixture.

Soak each piece of bread in the egg mixture till the entire slice is covered with the custard.

Place the cornflakes on a plate, press each piece of bread into the cornflake mixture.

Preheat Flip Pan over medium for 2–3 minutes per side, then spray with nonstick spray.

Place each cornflake encrusted piece of bread on the griddle side.

Cook for 4 then flip and cook for 3 minutes longer or till golden brown and cooked through.

Serve hot with maple syrup and butter. Dust with powdered sugar.

NUTRITION FACTS

Serving Size: ¼ of a recipe

AMOUNT PER SERVING	% DAILY VALUE
Calories: 93	5%
Calories from Fat: 10	1%
Total Fat: 1g	2%
Saturated Fat: 1g	5%
Cholesterol: 38mg	13%
Sodium: 313mg	13%
Total Carbohydrates: 18g	6%
Fiber: 0g	0%
Sugars: 6g	
Protein: 3g	5%
Vitamin A:	2%
Vitamin C:	1%
Calcium:	3%
Iron:	15%

Pumpkin Pie French Toast

Serves 6

INGREDIENTS

12 slices whole wheat sandwich bread
3 eggs
½ cup milk
¾ cup pumpkin purée
1 teaspoon pumpkin pie spice
butter and syrup for serving

DIRECTIONS

In a medium mixing bowl, whisk together the eggs, milk, pumpkin and pie spice until smooth.

Dip each side of the bread and soak for several minutes.

Preheat Flip Pan top and bottom on medium heat.

Spray well with nonstick spray.

Place 4 slices of bread in the Flip Pan at a time, close Flip Pan and cook for 2 minutes, then flip and cook for two minutes longer.

Repeat with the remaining slices.

Once all are cooked, serve with butter and maple syrup.

NUTRITION FACTS

Serving Size: ⅙ of a recipe

AMOUNT PER SERVING	% DAILY VALUE
Calories: 204	10%
Calories from Fat: 38	6%
Total Fat: 4g	6%
Saturated Fat: 1g	5%
Cholesterol: 73mg	24%
Sodium: 353mg	15%
Total Carbohydrates: 33g	11%
Fiber: 3g	12%
Sugars: 6g	
Protein: 7g	13%
Vitamin A:	93%
Vitamin C:	0%
Calcium:	8%
Iron:	14%

Maple Bacon Stuffed French Toast

Serves 2

Divine perfection! Creamy salty crunchy sweet!

INGREDIENTS

4 eggs

¼ cup milk

1 teaspoon cinnamon, divided

dash of nutmeg

½ teaspoon vanilla

4 slices of bacon, cooked and crumbled

4 ounces cream cheese at room temp

2 tablespoons maple syrup

8 slices French bread

DIRECTIONS

Cook bacon till crispy, then crumble or chop into small pieces.

Beat the cream cheese till smooth, then beat in the maple syrup. Test the flavor, add more syrup if desired. Fold in the crumbled bacon with a rubber spatula. Set aside.

Cut 4 slices of French bread about 2½ inches thick and butterfly each slice. In an 8×8 baking dish, crack the eggs and add ½ of the cinnamon. Mix carefully with a fork. When cinnamon is mixed in add the vanilla and nutmeg and stir again. Add the milk and stir. Fill the bread with the cream cheese filling. Soak the stuffed breads in the egg mixture. Soak for at least 5 minutes per side.

Spray the Flip Pan well with nonstick spray. Preheat Flip Pan top and bottom over medium heat. Place the soaked bread in the Flip Pan. Cook for 3 minutes flip then cook for 3 minutes longer.

Remove to platter to keep warm. Serve with warmed maple syrup and additional crumbled bacon.

NUTRITION FACTS

Serving Size: ½ of a recipe

AMOUNT PER SERVING	% DAILY VALUE
Calories: 110	6%
Calories from Fat: 59	9%
Total Fat: 7g	11%
Saturated Fat: 2g	10%
Cholesterol: 289mg	96%
Sodium: 102mg	4%
Total Carbohydrates: 2g	1%
Fiber: 0g	0%
Sugars: 2g	
Protein: 9g	16%
Vitamin A:	9%
Vitamin C:	1%
Calcium:	6%
Iron:	5%

Original Flip Pan
Hearty One-Pot Meals

Chicken Enchilada Casserole

Serves 6

INGREDIENTS

enchiladas

4 cups shredded deli rotisserie chicken

9 slices bacon, crisply cooked and crumbled

1 packet (1 oz.) ranch dressing & seasoning mix

1 pouch (8 oz.) roasted tomato Mexican cooking sauce

2 cups (8 oz.) shredded Mexican blend cheese

20 flour tortillas (6-inch) for soft tacos

sauce

2 tablespoons olive oil

½ cup chopped onion

1 can (4.5 oz.) chopped green chilies

2 tablespoons all-purpose flour

2 cups chicken broth

1 cup sour cream

garnishes, as desired:

    fresh cilantro, chopped

    fresh tomato, chopped

    red onion, chopped

NUTRITION FACTS

Serving Size: ⅙ of a recipe

AMOUNT PER SERVING	% DAILY VALUE
Calories: 440	22%
Calories from Fat: 165	25%
Total Fat: 18g	28%
Saturated Fat: 7g	35%
Cholesterol: 44mg	15%
Sodium: 973mg	41%
Total Carbohydrates: 8g	3%
Fiber: 0g	0%
Sugars: 1g	
Protein: 16g	29%
Vitamin A:	6%
Vitamin C:	9%
Calcium:	3%
Iron:	1%

Heat oven to 350°F.

In large bowl, mix chicken, half of the crumbled bacon, 1 tablespoon of the ranch dressing & seasoning mix, the cooking sauce, and 1 cup of the cheese; mix well. Divide mixture among tortillas, and roll up, placing seam side down on a parchment lined cutting board.

Preheat Flip Pan over medium heat about 2 minutes

Add the oil and heat. Cook onion in oil until softened. Add chilies, and cook until most of the liquid from chilies evaporates. Stir in flour. Slowly add chicken broth, stirring constantly to prevent lumps.

Once broth is incorporated, cook another minute or until slightly thickened. Stir in sour cream and remaining ranch dressing & seasoning mix, and simmer 1 minute with Flip Pan closed.

Add the rolled tortillas to the sauce Top with remaining cheese and bacon.

Bake without lid 20 minutes until cheese is melted and sauce is bubbling.

Cool 5 minutes before serving with garnishes.

Cheesy Potato Breakfast Casserole

INGREDIENTS

1 pound mild Italian sausage, sliced thin

1 yellow onion, chopped

7 eggs

½ cup milk

3 cups potatoes, diced

8-ounce brick of mild Cheddar cheese, grated

salt and pepper, to taste

DIRECTIONS

Preheat oven to 350.

Preheat Flip Pan top and bottom over medium high heat

Add sausage and onions and potatoes close lid and cook for minutes per side.

Drain the fat.

In a large mixing bowl, combine the eggs milk cheese and salt and pepper.

Pour into Flip Pan over sausage potatoes

Allow casserole to rest for 15–20 minutes.

Cook Time: 35 minutes

NUTRITION FACTS

Serving Size: ⅛ of a recipe

AMOUNT PER SERVING	% DAILY VALUE
Calories: 338	17%
Calories from Fat: 222	33%
Total Fat: 25g	38%
Saturated Fat: 12g	60%
Cholesterol: 190mg	63%
Sodium: 631mg	26%
Total Carbohydrates: 9g	3%
Fiber: 1g	4%
Sugars: 1g	
Protein: 12g	22%
Vitamin A:	10%
Vitamin C:	6%
Calcium:	24%
Iron:	5%

Chicken Florentine Spaghetti Squash

Serves 1

INGREDIENTS

1 frozen chicken tender
½ teaspoon olive oil
2 cups spinach
1 ripe tomato, diced
½ teaspoon garlic salt
pinch basil
½ teaspoon crushed red pepper flakes
1 cup cooked spaghetti squash, instructions below

DIRECTIONS

Pre heat Flip Pan top and bottom.

Add the chicken tender and close the lid. Cook for 5 minutes per side.

Remove the chicken to a cutting board.

Add the oil and heat for 2 minutes.

I cook my spaghetti squash in the Flip Pan 25 minutes split in half with ½ cup chicken stock. Then scoop out.

Add the chicken and all the other ingredients.

Cook for 3 minutes per side.

NUTRITION FACTS

Serving Size: 1 of a recipe

AMOUNT PER SERVING	% DAILY VALUE
Calories: 269	13%
Calories from Fat: 45	7%
Total Fat: 5g	8%
Saturated Fat: 0g	2%
Cholesterol: 90mg	30%
Sodium: 1423mg	59%
Total Carbohydrates: 10g	3%
Fiber: 4g	17%
Sugars: 0g	0%
Protein: 52g	95%
Vitamin A:	20%
Vitamin C:	42%
Calcium:	0%
Iron:	6%

Ginger Stir Fry Sauce

I love this as the sauce for the Cantonese Shrimp

INGREDIENTS

½ cup chicken stock

3 tablespoons soy sauce

1 tablespoon sherry

1 tablespoon sugar

1 teaspoon cornstarch dissolved in 1 tablespoon of orange juice

1 teaspoon rice wine vinegar

2 tablespoons sesame oil

3 tablespoons fresh ginger, grated

DIRECTIONS

In a bowl mix the stock, soy sauce, sherry and cornstarch and vinegar. Set aside

Place the sauce pan onto burner, on medium

Add the sesame oil and ginger and cook for 2 minutes careful not to burn.

Add the ingredients from the bowl to the sauce pan, bring to a boil stirring till thickened.

NUTRITION FACTS

Serving Size: ¼ of a recipe

AMOUNT PER SERVING	% DAILY VALUE
Calories: 96	5%
Calories from Fat: 61	9%
Total Fat: 7g	11%
Saturated Fat: 1g	5%
Cholesterol: 0mg	0%
Sodium: 511mg	21%
Total Carbohydrates: 7g	2%
Fiber: 0g	0%
Sugars: 6g	
Protein: 2g	4%
Vitamin A:	1%
Vitamin C:	1%
Calcium:	1%
Iron:	0%

Nevar's Shrimp Pad Thai

Serves 2

INGREDIENTS

4 tablespoons lime juice
3 tablespoons fish sauce
3 tablespoons sugar
1 tablespoon chili sauce
6 ounces rice noodles
1 tablespoon peanut oil
6 ounces shrimp
2 shallots, chopped
2 cloves garlic, chopped
1 egg, lightly beaten
2 tablespoons roasted peanuts, chopped
1 cup bean sprouts
2 green onions, sliced
¼ cup cilantro, chopped
1 lime, cut into wedges

NUTRITION FACTS

Serving Size: ½ of a recipe

AMOUNT PER SERVING	% DAILY VALUE
Calories: 698	35%
Calories from Fat: 188	28%
Total Fat: 22g	34%
Saturated Fat: 4g	20%
Cholesterol: 185mg	62%
Sodium: 2110mg	88%
Total Carbohydrates: 100g	33%
Fiber: 2g	8%
Sugars: 23g	
Protein: 24g	44%
Vitamin A:	32%
Vitamin C:	236%
Calcium:	7%
Iron:	46%

DIRECTIONS

Place a sauce pan on medium high burner

Add the lime juice, fish sauce, sugar and chili sauce and stir until the sugar is dissolved. Remove from heat and set aside

Soak the rice noodles in water as directed on package until just pliable.

Add oil to the Flip Pan.

When the oil and pot are hot, carefully add the shrimp, shallots and garlic and sauté for 2–3 minutes with lid closed.

Add the sauce and the noodles and mix well.

Add the egg let it sit a moment, stir then close the lid and cook for 1 minute.

Add the peanuts and bean sprouts and cook for a minute longer with lid closed.

Garnish with green onions and cilantro. Serve with lime wedges.

Stove Top Lasagna

INGREDIENTS

1 small onion, chopped

3 cloves garlic, minced

1 teaspoon olive oil

1 small zucchini, shredded

1 28-ounce can san Marzano diced tomatoes (my favorite)

pinch sea salt

pinch black pepper

2 leaves basil, rolled and chopped thin

5 pieces oven ready lasagna noodles

1 cup ricotta cheese

1 cup shredded mozzarella cheese, divided

½ cup Parmesan cheese, divided

2 large eggs, beaten

pinch nutmeg

¼ cup chicken stock

NUTRITION FACTS

Serving Size: ¼ of a recipe

AMOUNT PER SERVING	% DAILY VALUE
Calories: 723	36%
Calories from Fat: 175	26%
Total Fat: 20g	31%
Saturated Fat: 11g	55%
Cholesterol: 128mg	43%
Sodium: 859mg	36%
Total Carbohydrates: 7g	2%
Fiber: 1g	4%
Sugars: 2g	
Protein: 32g	58%
Vitamin A:	16%
Vitamin C:	5%
Calcium:	81%
Iron:	1%

DIRECTIONS

Place the Flip Pan on medium heat.

Add the onion and start to cook add the garlic zucchini and oil and cook till tender with lid open. About 2 minutes.

Add the tomatoes and season with salt pepper and basil.

Close lid and let cook for 5 minutes.

Mix the ricotta with ½ the mozzarella and Parmesan, add in the eggs and nutmeg.

Open the Flip Pan and ladle out half of the sauce.

Place 3 pieces of lasagna on the sauce.

Spoon the ricotta mixture over the noodles.

Top with more noodles.

Pour remaining sauce in and top with the remaining mozzarella and Parmesan.

Pour in the stock, close the lid and cook over medium 30 minutes.

Unstuffed Cabbage

INGREDIENTS

1½ pounds extra lean ground beef

1 tablespoon olive oil

1 large onion, chopped

2 cloves garlic, minced

1 small head of cabbage, chopped

1 28-ounce can petite diced tomatoes

½ cup tomato sauce

½ cup beef stock

1 teaspoon black pepper

1 teaspoon sea salt

DIRECTIONS

Place Flip Pan on stove preheat top and bottom for 2–3 minutes.

Add olive oil and heat for 2 minutes.

Add ground beef and onion and cook, stirring until ground beef is no longer pink and onion is tender.

Add garlic and continue cooking for 1 minute with lid closed.

Add the chopped cabbage, tomatoes, tomato sauce stock, pepper and salt.

Close the lid and simmer for 20 to 30 minutes, or until the cabbage is tender.

NUTRITION FACTS

Serving Size: ¼ of a recipe

AMOUNT PER SERVING	% DAILY VALUE
Calories: 368	18%
Calories from Fat: 83	12%
Total Fat: 30g	46%
Saturated Fat: 18g	90%
Cholesterol: 114mg	38%
Sodium: 976mg	41%
Total Carbohydrates: 3g	1%
Fiber: 1g	4%
Sugars: 2g	
Protein: 35g	64%
Vitamin A:	3%
Vitamin C:	10%
Calcium:	0%
Iron:	19%

Original Flip Pan
Sandwiches

Buffalo Chicken
Grilled Cheese Sandwich

Serves 2

INGREDIENTS

1 large boneless, skinless chicken breast

nonstick spray

salt and pepper

1 cup wing sauce

4 slices garlic bread (or Texas toast)

4 slices pepper jack cheese

2 ounces blue cheese or gorgonzola cheese crumbles

2 tablespoons mayonnaise

DIRECTIONS

Preheat Flip Pan top and bottom over medium high heat. Spray the Flip Pan with nonstick spray

Season the chicken breast with salt and pepper. Add the chicken breast to the Flip Pan and cook the chicken breast for 4 minutes per side.

Remove the chicken breast to a cutting board. Let rest for a few minutes. Then slice super thin. Wipe the Flip Pan and remove from heat while assembling the sandwiches.

In a medium bowl stir together the sliced chicken breast and wing sauce. Spread ½ tablespoon of mayonnaise on one side of each slice of the bread, then stack mayo sides together. Layer one slice Pepper Jack on each bread stack, then dollop of hot sauce slathered chicken breast and then 1 ounce of blue cheese crumbles.

Place bread mayo side down in preheated Flip Pan over medium heat. Close Flip Pan and let cook for 3–4 minutes or until golden flip and cook 2–3 minutes longer.

Cook Time: 20 minutes

NUTRITION FACTS

Serving Size: ½ of a recipe

AMOUNT PER SERVING	% DAILY VALUE
Calories: 127	6%
Calories from Fat: 107	16%
Total Fat: 12g	18%
Saturated Fat: 2g	10%
Cholesterol: 19mg	6%
Sodium: 154mg	6%
Total Carbohydrates: 0g	0%
Fiber: 0g	0%
Sugars: 0g	0%
Protein: 5g	9%
Vitamin A:	0%
Vitamin C:	0%
Calcium:	0%
Iron:	1%

Cuban Sandwich

Toasted and Tasty!!

INGREDIENTS

1 loaf Cuban bread
1 ounce regular mustard
1 ounce mayonnaise
4 horizontal slices of dill pickles
½ pound sliced deli ham, shaved
¼ pound roast pork, sliced
¼ imported Swiss cheese, sliced thin
1 ounce butter

DIRECTIONS

Cut Cuban bread to desired size, common size is 7 inches. Next, slice open the bread down the middle. Mix the mayonnaise and mustard together. On the topside of the bread spread 1-ounce of mustard mixture, evenly across. Then place 4 pickles on top of the mustard. You then place the Swiss cheese on top of the pickles. Cover with ham evenly on bottom of bread. On top of the ham, place slices of roast pork. You then join both halves of the sandwich. You are now ready to cook your Cuban sandwich.

Preheat Flip Pan top and bottom for 2–3 minutes per side over medium heat.

Spread butter on top of the bread evenly. Place the sandwich in the Flip Pan and close. Cook 3 minutes per side.

Remove to a cutting board, and press the sandwich with the Flip Pan to flatten.

Cut diagonally.

NUTRITION FACTS

Serving Size: ½ of a recipe

AMOUNT PER SERVING	% DAILY VALUE
Calories: 1143	57%
Calories from Fat: 123	18%
Total Fat: 13g	20%
Saturated Fat: 0g	0%
Cholesterol: 174mg	58%
Sodium: 1894mg	79%
Total Carbohydrates: 135g	45%
Fiber: 9g	36%
Sugars: 18g	
Protein: 68g	124%
Vitamin A:	3%
Vitamin C:	0%
Calcium:	18%
Iron:	54%

French Onion Grilled Cheese Sandwiches

INGREDIENTS

3 tablespoons mayonnaise

1 tablespoon olive oil

2 medium yellow onions, sliced ¼ inch thick

1 teaspoon kosher, salt

½ teaspoon black pepper

1 teaspoon sugar

1 teaspoon fresh thyme leaves

3 tablespoons beef stock

4 slices sourdough bread

½ cup gruyere cheese

DIRECTIONS

Preheat Flip Pan on medium high heat top and bottom. Add the butter and olive and let butter melt. Add in the onions and stir so they are coated in all the fat. Close lid and let cook for 5 minutes.

Stir and add in the salt, pepper, sugar and thyme. Stir, close lid and cook for 5 minutes longer.

Add in the stock scrape any bits that accumulated on the bottom of the Flip Pan. Close lid and cook 2 minutes longer. Place onions in another bowl.

Rinse and wipe down Flip Pan then place back on burner to preheat over medium.

Spread mayonnaise on one side of each slice of bread, place mayo side down in Flip Pan, and top it with a little shredded Gruyere. Add half of the onion mixture and then more of the cheese. Top with a second slice of bread mayo side up.

Close Flip Pan and cook for 3 minutes, open make sure sandwiches are golden brown and stacked well and cook for 2 minutes longer.

Cut in half and serve.

NUTRITION FACTS

Serving Size: ½ of a recipe

AMOUNT PER SERVING	% DAILY VALUE
Calories: 85	4%
Calories from Fat: 66	10%
Total Fat: 8g	12%
Saturated Fat: 1g	5%
Cholesterol: 7mg	2%
Sodium: 1233mg	51%
Total Carbohydrates: 2g	1%
Fiber: 0g	0%
Sugars: 2g	
Protein: 3g	5%
Vitamin A:	0%
Vitamin C:	0%
Calcium:	0%
Iron:	3%

Italian Beef Sandwiches

INGREDIENTS

1 3-pound cooked Pot Roast, page 63
4 green bell peppers, seeded and cut into strips
nonstick spray
1 teaspoon granulated garlic
kosher salt and freshly ground black pepper
½ cup giardiniera spicy pickled vegetables
6 soft sub or hoagie rolls, sliced lengthwise
1 tablespoon mayonnaise
6 slices provolone cheese (optional)

DIRECTIONS

Preheat the Flip Pan top and bottom over medium heat.

Spray with nonstick spray and add the bell pepper. Close and cook for 2 minutes.

Add the pot roast and the seasoning and Giardinera.

Close lid and cook for 4 minutes per side till meat is heated through and penetrated with the spicy flavor of the pickled veggies.

Remove the meat mixture to a bowl, and clean Flip Pan.

Reheat Flip Pan over medium heat.

Smear mayonnaise all over the outside of the rolls and fill each bun with meat and top with cheese. Place 2 at a time in Flip Pan and cook for 2 minutes per side to heat and toast the roll and melt the cheese.

Serve with a little dish of the spicy jus on the side.

NUTRITION FACTS

Serving Size: ⅙ of a recipe

AMOUNT PER SERVING	% DAILY VALUE
Calories: 117	6%
Calories from Fat: 87	13%
Total Fat: 10g	15%
Saturated Fat: 5g	25%
Cholesterol: 26mg	9%
Sodium: 265mg	11%
Total Carbohydrates: 0g	0%
Fiber: 0g	0%
Sugars: 0g	0%
Protein: 8g	15%
Vitamin A:	6%
Vitamin C:	0%
Calcium:	25%
Iron:	0%

Prosciutto Blackberry Brie Croissants

Serves 2

INGREDIENTS

2 large croissants, sliced in half
2 tablespoons blackberry preserves
1 small pear, sliced thin
4 slices brie
1 tablespoon of butter
4 slices prosciutto
½ cup baby arugula

DIRECTIONS

Preheat the Flip Pan top and bottom over medium heat.

Assemble each sandwich first by spreading blackberry preserves on the bottom of croissant, top with 4 pear slices then Brie then prosciutto.

Place the top of the croissant on the sandwich and butter each sandwich well on the outside.

Place the sandwich in the Flip Pan, Cook for 3 minutes, then flip and cook for 3 minutes longer.

Remove to cutting board and allow to cool.

Add the arugula if using

NUTRITION FACTS

Serving Size: ½ of a recipe

AMOUNT PER SERVING	% DAILY VALUE
Calories: 149	7%
Calories from Fat: 50	8%
Total Fat: 6g	9%
Saturated Fat: 0g	0%
Cholesterol: 15mg	5%
Sodium: 60mg	3%
Total Carbohydrates: 15g	5%
Fiber: 2g	8%
Sugars: 9g	
Protein: 0g	0%
Vitamin A:	4%
Vitamin C:	5%
Calcium:	1%
Iron:	1%

Grilled Mac n Cheese
with Bacon and Tomato

Serves 4

INGREDIENTS

4 cups cooked Easy Macaroni and Cheese, page 75
8 slices potato bread smeared with mayonnaise on both sides
4 slices American cheese
8 slices thick-cut smoked bacon, cooked crisp
1 large ripe tomato (preferably heirloom), cut ¼ inch thick

DIRECTIONS

Evenly spread the Easy Mac and Cheese in an 8-inch square baking dish. Cover the dish with plastic wrap and refrigerate until firm, about 1 hour. Cut the mac and cheese into 4 equal-size squares.

Preheat a Flip Pan top and bottom over medium heat.

Place each mac and cheese square on a slice of bread, top with 1 slice American cheese and 2 slices bacon. Top with a second piece of bread and place two sandwich at a time in the Flip Pan cook for 3 minutes flip and then cook 3 minutes longer.

Repeat with the remaining ingredients.

Add the tomato slice on top of the bacon after cooking before cutting in half.

NUTRITION FACTS

Serving Size: ¼ of a recipe

AMOUNT PER SERVING	% DAILY VALUE
Calories: 139	7%
Calories from Fat: 100	15%
Total Fat: 11g	17%
Saturated Fat: 5g	25%
Cholesterol: 25mg	8%
Sodium: 463mg	19%
Total Carbohydrates: 4g	1%
Fiber: 0g	0%
Sugars: 1g	
Protein: 7g	13%
Vitamin A:	9%
Vitamin C:	10%
Calcium:	10%
Iron:	1%

Monte Cristo Sandwich

INGREDIENTS

6 slices white bread (I like potato bread)
2 tablespoons mayonnaise
4 slices jarlsburg cheese
2 slices turkey breast
2 slices black forest ham
3 large eggs, beaten
¼ cup milk
nonstick spray

DIRECTIONS

On a work surface, lay out 4 slices of bread and spread with mayonnaise top and bottom. Top each slice with the 1 slice of cheese and 1 slice of turkey and one slice of ham. Put the third slice of bread on top of one stack, and flip the remaining stack on top, cheese-side down, to make two triple-decker sandwich.

Using a knife, cut the crusts off the sandwich (this helps to pinch and seal the ends). Wrap the sandwich tightly with plastic wrap and refrigerate for at least 30 minutes and up to 6 hours.

Combine the eggs and milk in a bowl. Preheat the Flip Pan top and bottom over medium-high heat. Unwrap the sandwich and dip it in the egg batter, to coat evenly. Spray Flip Pan well with nonstick spray. Gently place the sandwiches in the Flip Pan. Close the lid and cook for 3 minutes. Flip then cook for 3 minutes longer.

Cut the Monte Cristo in ½, transfer it to a plate. Serve hot.

NUTRITION FACTS

Serving Size: ½ of a recipe

AMOUNT PER SERVING	% DAILY VALUE
Calories: 86	4%
Calories from Fat: 46	7%
Total Fat: 5g	8%
Saturated Fat: 2g	10%
Cholesterol: 218mg	73%
Sodium: 81mg	3%
Total Carbohydrates: 2g	1%
Fiber: 0g	0%
Sugars: 2g	
Protein: 7g	13%
Vitamin A:	7%
Vitamin C:	1%
Calcium:	6%
Iron:	4%

Rueben Sandwich

My favorite sandwich ever!!

INGREDIENTS

4 slices of marble rye bread
1 tablespoon mayonnaise
4 slices Swiss cheese
½ pound pastrami or corned beef, shaved thin
2 tablespoons thousand island dressing
¼ cup of sauerkraut, drained

DIRECTIONS

Smear mayonnaise on one side of all the slices of bread. This will be the outside of the sandwich.

Place two slices of bread mayonnaise side down, divide the meat between the two pieces of bread.

Add the dressing and sauerkraut, then top with the cheese, and the remaining two slices of bread, mayonnaise side up.

Preheat the Flip Pan over medium heat 2–3 minutes per side.

Add the sandwiches to the pan. Close and cook for 3 minutes then flip and cook 3 minutes longer.

If a deeper color is desired cook for a few minutes longer.

NUTRITION FACTS

Serving Size: ½ of a recipe

AMOUNT PER SERVING	% DAILY VALUE
Calories: 737	37%
Calories from Fat: 397	60%
Total Fat: 44g	68%
Saturated Fat: 21g	105%
Cholesterol: 166mg	55%
Sodium: 1335mg	56%
Total Carbohydrates: 28g	9%
Fiber: 3g	12%
Sugars: 1g	
Protein: 57g	104%
Vitamin A:	20%
Vitamin C:	2%
Calcium:	84%
Iron:	21%

Alphabetical
Index